FACING EAST: BOARDING SCHOOL & BEYOND

A K-5 NAVAJO MEMOIR

Copyright © 2025 by Evelyn Begody

For permission to use material from *Facing East*

ISBN: 979-8-9910203-9-8 (Paperback)

ISBN: 979-8-9910203-2-9 (Ebook)

please contact

begayevelyn@gmail.com.

Begody Books POBox 4542 Gallup, NM 87305

No AI Training is permitted in using any of the content. No AI was used in the writing this memoir.

Cover and Book Design: brenda@triomarketers.com

Photographs: Evelyn Begody

Publisher's Cataloging-in-Publication Data

Subjects: Evelyn Begody. | Indigenous: Navajo. | Education. | Memoir. | Public Educators. |

Thank you for buying an authorized edition of *Facing East*. To honor Indigenous writers and copyright laws, please do not copy, scan, or distribute without written permission. Countless warrior women and children have sacrificed their lives for you to hold this book in your hands. Your readership is beyond invaluable. *Ahehee.*

FACING EAST: BOARDING SCHOOL & BEYOND

A K-5 NAVAJO MEMOIR

❧❦

EVELYN BEGODY

EDUCATORS' COMMENTS & REVIEWS

As an indie author, I oversee the presentation of my books. When I discussed this book with colleagued/ friends, I asked several if they would like to write a blurb for me. My intention was to get early reviews, but I also wanted to acknowledge the sweat of the earth educators. Educators get scarce recognition, if any. Since this memoir honors my primary and intermediate educator-leaders, I thought I'd share some current educators' comments after reading excerpts of *Facing East*.

༺❦༻

"Although I'm a non-Dine speaker, Begody's description of her family dynamics have something in common with my own family and with many families I've worked with over the years. Her story feels relatable even though it's uniquely her own life. What I take away is how resilient she was as a child; she focuses on the values her family instilled in her and the unintentional lessons received from her parents' choices & their relationship with each other. Evelyn Begody invites the reader to see the positive influences of the public education system and her experience of 2nd grade from her 2nd grade self's perspective. I enjoy memoirs of people from different walks of life. She packs a whole lot into this chapter; it's a lot, but I enjoyed reading it."

Sarah Booth, K-8 ESS & General Education, 16 years

"Begody has interwoven her personal narrative of youthful curiosity, growth, and struggle with the hindsight of an accomplished educator. Her stories paint a rich atmosphere of the hot sun, dusty Phoenix streets, and cool patios. I connected with the keen observations of an imaginative and introspective child, and the escape she found in reading and drawing. Evelyn Begody's book should be read by all educators interacting with Indigenous students and working within Indigenous communities."

Rachel Brown, Art Educator, 6 years

"A wonderfully explicit presentation of a young girl's realization of the dynamics of relationships and human growth. Absorbing narrative with light humor sprinkled among the harsh realities of life events, including human bias and unkindness. Details and examples provide the reader with an opportunity to be in 5th grade at Emerson Elementary School."

Ella Earl, ELA Educator, 27 years

"From the awe of seeing new, exciting aspects of life to the quiet rituals of weekend visits with grandparents, this book captures how moments of wonder, fear, and family tradition shape a child's inner world. The contrasts between parents are interwoven with the transformative influence of school, where a teacher becomes both motivator and angel, igniting confidence through learning. This book resonates as both a deeply personal memoir and a universal meditation on how children make sense of love, culture, and learning."

Wendy Guess, PhD

"The intertwined stories of Evelyn Begody's reservation life and her urban life offer insight into her upbringing. The incorporation of her Navajo culture into her urban life entailed the presence of her mother's imperishable connection with Rez Life. This allowed me to reflect on my own life as I compared how I grew up on the reservation and how she grew up with unique opportunities."

Leah Kayonnie, ELA Educator, 6 years

"Evelyn Begody's writing is like no other: smart, imaginative, startlingly honest, deeply engaged with the world and its mysteries. To read her is to see one's own world differently."

Lucy Maddox, *The People of Rose Hill: Black and White Life on a Maryland Plantation.*

"This book took me back to moments so familiar they felt like memories from my own childhood growing up. The author's vivid descriptions of the warmth of the sun on bare arms, the wind tossing hair, and the quiet strength found in family traditions made me feel as if I were there, riding in the back of that pickup truck, fully immersed in those simple but powerful moments. The deep connection to Navajo culture throughout the story reminded me of values I hold close: respect for family, the land, and the stories that shape who we are. Watching a mother learn to drive despite many challenges and imagining the vast beauty of Glen Canyon Dam along with the enormous fish beneath its surface stirred a mix of awe, respect, and a profound sense of belonging that goes beyond place. The book made me reflect on how culture is not just something passed down but the very heartbeat that teaches resilience, hope, and love through every struggle and triumph. This story felt like a bridge between worlds and a reminder that no matter where we come from, the threads of family, faith, and courage connect us all."

Carwin Murillo, ELA Educator, 16 years

"This book captivated me with its powerful storytelling and lyrical prose. The author, a Navajo woman, writes with the skill and depth of a true wordsmith—each sentence carefully crafted. I found myself unable to put it down, eagerly turning page after page, hungry for the full journey she lays before the reader.

Though the book courageously explores difficult topics such as abuse and rape, the author handles them with extraordinary care and nuance. Her writing never feels gratuitous or overwhelming. Instead, it is grounding, respectful, and allows space for readers to engage without being triggered. There's a strength in her voice that both acknowledges trauma and honors resilience.

One of the many things I appreciated was her seamless integration of Navajo words and expressions throughout the narrative. Rather than placing definitions in a glossary at the back—disrupting the flow of reading—she includes them within the text itself. This choice not only enriches the reading experience but also invites the reader into her culture in a way that feels intimate and respectful.

This book is compelling— A testament to survival, identity, and the power of storytelling, it's the kind of work that stays with you long after the last page. I can't wait to read more from this incredible author."

Ann Wasilewski, ELA Educator, 36 year

AUTHOR'S NOTE

This memoir attempts to capture a long ago starting with my family's arrival to Oakland, when I was very young. Some of the gaps were filled by my octogenarian dad, whose memories are crisply sharp but fuzzy about some. I know this early period holds him still because he sometimes says, "I'll move there and live under the cold Oakland sun." He means this in the best of hearts.

I have renamed people, but a few I kept the real names. I have remained true to the events as I remember. I know I've made mistakes because memory is a slippery, fickle abstract.

This memoir was designed for healing. I'm in my 60s now, and to embitter the past with complaints isn't the path of this book.

DEDICATION

To my dear late husband Bo,

my teachers, my professors,

Jim & Lucy Maddox,

my students,

my colleagues,

my dear K-5 peers.

CONTENTS

Preface 1

Chapter 1   Kindergarten: Sunny El Monte 5

Chapter 2   First Grade: The White House 25

Chapter 3   Second Grade: Moby Dick 81

Chapter 4   Third Grade: Two Different Teachers 119

Chapter 5   Fourth Grade: Train and Boxcars Journey ... 179

Chapter 6   Fifth Grade: Loss and Learning 229

Afterword 263

Gratitude & Acknowledgment 265

An excerpt from *The Spirit of Work* 269

Campsite Clerk: 269

PREFACE

I started this project during Covid, an awful year-and-a-quarter during which I was reluctant to call myself an educator because the title felt fraudulent. Teachers used Zoom in a community where Internet was shaky at best, and my desktop screen often darkened. How desperately I rebooted and reconnected and attempted to breathe life into that Zoom call, with fewer students each time.

I really believed I could continue teaching as usual. I couldn't, of course. My students initially kept up with our novel, *Frankenstein*, but more and more dropped from the Zoom. Covid brought out our best and worst. Some seniors came to our online class and diligently wrote responses to their reading, prefacing them with a casual I-think-this-is-what-you-want-Begody, before diving into their ideas, comparisons, and connections. I was dismayed to see formerly thesis-driven writing lose heft and substance, dwindle, and drift off. I snatched at remnants of learning, strained every inch of my five feet to grab and swipe desperately, but failed to grasp what had been lost.

I formed a book club of teachers and a cognitive coach, hoping to smooth the jagged edges of poor teaching. We read health books, brain retraining books, trauma and education books, and wonderful, hopeful Isabel Wilkerson's *Caste: The Origin of Our Discontents*. The latter hit home for me. It made sense we were going through an educational de-revolution of sorts—a shift that would greatly alter schools and education itself.

Today, while we no longer keep a sandwich bag of extra masks on hand, and we now fly with clearly unwiped trays in the main cabin, and a cough is just a cough, the effects of that year-and-a-quarter exile from our classrooms still resound. Reading has plummeted. Homework, admittedly less often assigned, is even more rarely done. Has this also affected my colleagues? Maybe. I dedicated 24 years to working in a remote, rural public high school serving a vast area where buses sometimes travel on washboard roads, dropping off students who then walk miles to humble homes with cattle in corrals, wood-burning stoves, and bread still made traditionally by hand. I grew up with an oil-burning lantern, an outhouse, and juniper wood burning in a crackling fire. Some of my students' homes were no different.

Though the landscape remains ever gorgeous with heart-arresting sunsets, students have changed. Motivation has waned. Ironically, while the educational bar of achievement rose for teachers, the bar dropped drastically for students: too many pass without demonstrating the skills they need. Some might argue that the deterioration has taken place over a decade or two, but I saw it most acutely during and post pandemic. I used to be the teacher who pushed hard for college, but once I saw the low reading levels, I stepped back. College textbooks are written at 1400 Lexile, and many of my students were finishing high school at eighth grade reading levels. To worsen the trend, libraries were converted to study halls, meeting places, media centers. Our dear school library imploded; books were relegated to a far-off room and hidden in corners, wooden bookshelves were dismantled, and the dirt-crusted carpet worn thin by happy feet of students searching for books was replaced. The book scents wafted out and educators forgot about the old library and the promises it held.

Even before this picture of educational slackening formed in my mind, I had begun writing about my own education to help me understand it. Originally, I had planned to write into my high school years, as I'd had an unusual education. I attended school in four states, all public but on and off the Navajo Nation, hence the reference to boarding school in my title. Although I'm a US citizen, I speak English as a second language, like many immigrants. I started school knowing very little English, which might have given me a healthy dose of imposter syndrome. If I did well, I called it luck; if I did poorly, I blamed the slippery quality of English. A no win dilemma. Thus, I turned to retracing my journey to grasp more clearly the meaning of learning.

Year after year, teachers braid together myriad tiny strands of thread, lassoing students one by one into class, using the same slender threads to coax willing learners to open up to the idea of possibility as a reality for themselves. They may not have outstanding scores or even convincing linear growth, but still these students come back the next day, the next, the following week and beyond. Something is happening the metrics can't account for I have seen it in my classes.

While I write in this memoir about six teachers who took particular care of me. I had so many more caring guides: music teachers, a Brownie troop leader, librarians, a temporary special education teacher, a principal I discovered was my boss when I became an instructional assistant. Still another principal from decades past became, in later years, my colleague's husband. There are so, so many others whose influence I haven't recognized here or connected to yet.

The six leaders in my memoir shaped me. They were, in the broadest sense, my surrogate parents, and that is how I saw them. I sometimes encourage my students to open their hearts to learn. I get odd looks, but I know this is true. No one can learn with a closed, pinched-off heart. I tell students to relax when they take their practice SAT tests, that lots can go wrong on tests, so I only ask for their best. Similarly, I sometimes do not give my students my best. Sometimes I get so driven by the next assessment that I focus too much on that. Sometimes I tell myself to enjoy a break and have students learn about painting and interpretations. Even my best is highly interpretational as well. But I know that even doing our best can be a herculean request, one that would be impossible were it not for the many teachers we encounter along the way.

I welcome your journey through my K-5 experience. I hope you will be reminded of how much we share.

CHAPTER 1

Kindergarten: Sunny El Monte

My parents were relatively small in stature. In an ancient photo, my dad appears compact, wearing a short-sleeved button up with a white undershirt peeping out, belted tapered pants and black Oxford shoes. He sports black sunglasses and a crew cut. He could be a university student, but standing next to him are my mom and brother and me. He stations himself a little off from us. I bridge the gap by posing closer to him than to my mom. I grin as a breeze lifts my hair. I'm wearing what at first glance is a plaid jumper over a blouse but is really a dress sewed to look like a jumper. I liked it because it covered my arms. My legs are knobby and my feet are pointed pigeon-toed. I wear black slip-ons that gnawed the back of my ankles even though I wore socks, thin socks that slipped down under my heels and that I often yanked out as I hurried to keep up with my dad.

My mom wears a lime-colored sleeveless A-line dress. Her netted stockings, thickly webbed and cool even by today's standards, descend into spiked heels. Her hair is a bouffant, puffed out in a hive that lets loose some longer strands to fall on her shoulders. She gazes into the camera with a faraway look that some might call expressionless, but that I observe in her quiet moments. She holds my brother's shoulders. Dean wears an orange plaid button-down and nondescript pants. He's chubby, with an expression of the-glass-is-always-full cheer. And why not? He rarely feels the earth under his feet because our mom carries him everywhere as my dad dust-devils ahead. I'm clowning to lessen the tension that is barely perceptible but ever-present.

In the picture, we stand on a dirt path with palm trees behind us. The absence of pavement might indicate that El Monte is still partly undeveloped; then again, my mom might have sought out a rare patch of Mother Earth for a family snapshot during our brisk walk.

Back then, before my dad had a driver's license, we were carless, but my parents kept a roof over our heads, though just barely. My folks were young. I don't recall riding city buses, but I know we used them. I do remember the occasional Yellow Cab because these brought us home from the grocery store laden with food. My brother and I spent the majority of our time with our mother. She was our foundation. If my dad said something, I glanced at my mom for confirmation. I learned to read her subtle body language this way.

One reason we lived in El Monte was because Bell, where we'd moved from, had unreliable city bus schedules. Dad said he often arrived early to the stop, but when the bus didn't arrive, he'd give up waiting and begin walking. That's when the bus showed up. Sometimes the bus wheezed to a standstill at the next stop or my dad made a dash for it and hoped someone would signal the driver to stop. Youth and slow public transportation may explain his trim figure in those old pictures.

In 1967, My dad accepted an opportunity to move us from our home near Gap, Arizona, to Oakland, California, for GED, courses that would qualify him to work towards certification in welding. This opportunity changed our lives. The program provided an apartment, training, and a small stipend. We took a Greyhound to Oakland to live in a bustling and clamorous apartment complex of single level buildings with wide sturdy porches shared by two families, but it was populated with many families like ours, Natives from the rez given a chance to get educational opportunities. Some call this forced assimilation funded by the government, but if that's the definition, then education, employment, living beyond the holy mountains are as well. My folks saw and much later I see this as an opportunity for us, our family.

Coming from where we did, this neighborhood was a perpetual carnival of fun for my brother and me. Finding playmates in the courtyard was as simple as opening the front door and skipping down two or three steps. My brother Dean was never far behind me as I raced for the noisy cluster of children. Lost amid a hive of shouting and laughing, we were free. Our young mother hadn t yet grown full-fledged maternal wings, so we flew from her often and easily.

I wish I remembered more than fragments of this time—scenes of raucous play and my mom corralling us back to the porch steps when we d wandered too far from her. I hadn't quite accepted my role as my brother's keeper yet, but I was cooperative and have little doubt that I oversaw him cheerfully from my short leash. My dad's was held by the BIA; his GED classes and his welding and blueprint courses took place two blocks from our home, only a brief walk for him. Other Navajo families, young like my parents, lived in this neighborhood. The families rented apartments like ours, small and often crowded.

My mom didn't know English, having never attended school. She was limited in this new setting, but when my parents managed to buy a small black and white TV, my mom was glued to it. She loved the magic of TV-land. Television well might have been her version of the powerful adult babysitter. She learned phrases and practiced quietly, and gradually she gained the ability to understand English, though speaking was an altogether different beast for her. We rarely spoke English in our home. As thin as the walls and door of that apartment were, our Navajo language sealed us from the outside world. I believe that's how we survived when so many displaced Natives experienced other outcomes. The ability to speak a mother language may keep another, more alienating world at bay. We can thank my mom s refusal to speak English bound us to our Navajo language and reinforced our identity.

Either I was too young to notice or I ignored the looks of non-Navajos when I spoke Dine. I used Navajo without any shame or hesitation. I asked questions, lots of questions. I had no boundaries in my role of observer. *Something smells here. What is that? How does that work? Let me try that.* If my dad used a tool I never saw before, I wanted to try it. I was hungry for answers. During our walks, I ran ahead to stroke a freshly manicured lawn with my hands. Or I caressed the plants or smelled the flowers. More often, I touched something and then sniffed my fingers. I was a nightmare of bad manners on public display. I learned early to get out of earshot of my mom's scolding or the sting of her rebuke. She could easily pinch my upper arm or swiftly pull my hair—anything she could reach to silence me. I don't recall these being huge violations because I continued exploring my curious world and always stayed ahead of my mom.

I sensed some difference between my family and non-Natives early on, but in part because I talked incessantly, I never stopped to wonder what it was. I had opinions about everything, and gladly shared them. This Southern California period endures in flashes as sunny and pleasant. The beauty of childhood, so powerful for me, eclipses much of what was not beautiful.

My dad read the local paper. Not a strong reader, he scanned only a few sections, and did a lot of page flipping. His lips moved and made whispery, secretive sounds. He often used a pencil to mark items, probably the classifieds. Later my mom used the newspapers to line the small trash cans. My dad also wrote letters to his sister Sadie and his mother in long hand. After he wrote a line or two, he blew on his fingers as if to cool them. Or maybe this was his thinking strategy. He had so much to share and he couldn't write fast enough. Since his recipients were both illiterate in English,

I'm sure my Uncle Kee Nez Begody, his older brother, read the letters, or perhaps the trading post manager did. Someone in turn wrote a response. TV-land and books sometimes depict people shielding their letters close to their bosoms and hurrying to read in privacy, but not in our household. If a letter arrived, my mom handed it to my dad after dinner, when he read and translated it into Navajo for all of us. My dad chuckled readily, and I'm sure we waited impatiently or joined his laughter before he shared the hilarity. For me, his laughing before sharing the content was fortuitous because the letters never equaled my anticipation. It wasn't that my dad withheld anything in his translation. It's just that generally the content was seriously dull: horseback riding accidents, lambing, branding, livestock. However, humdrum as they might be, written communications reminded me of my extended family: my maternal grandparents, the many aunts and uncles from my mom s side, my single paternal grandmother and my aunt and uncles from my dad s side. We had countless cousins that I looked on as my brothers and sisters. Ma Bell hadn t arrived at our home yet and wouldn t until 1974. All we had were painstakingly penned letters that flew back and forth between Oakland and Gap, Arizona.

My mom took a picture of my brother and me. He's perched on a stuffed toy tiger, bigger than him, and I'm standing next to him in front of a TV on a stand. My eyes glisten. On very close inspection, I look like I've been crying, but I don't recall why.

Chapter 1 - Kindergarten: Sunny El Monte

We lived in Oakland for over a year, and for that time my brother and I remained close to my mom's side. She never showed genuine trust in this new world: our neighbors, the English language, common foods like mac and cheese, TV dinners, and the variety of *biligaana* food. To others, TV dinners meant eating in front of the television set, but my mom didn't permit that. Maybe a radio played at times, but not during meals. She trusted her cooking, the four of us in our small apartment, and our language. She also had that youthful energy that has fueled so many over time and through great difficulty. She would carry my brother while I tagged along beside her. Lifting and carrying was easy for her, as she had been accustomed to breaking and riding horses, herding sheep, hauling water in a horse-drawn wagon, animal butchering, and chopping wood. She was strong, summoning more strength whenever it was needed.

When my dad finished his welding courses, he and my mom decided to move us to Bell, in southeast Los Angeles. There I recall a magical bed that disappeared into the wall. The Murphy bed filled me with agitation and wonder. I saw my mom straighten the bed, and then in a single swoop, the bed disappeared into the wall. My mom had another amazing trick: She turned her back to us, and facing the counter and stove, she made food that she arranged on a plate or common serving dish where we dipped handmade bread before eating. Magic. We certainly never went hungry. My brother was a kid who savored food. So did I. Much later when I heard my friends brag that their moms were great cooks, I simply nodded, assuming everyone's mom was an unrecognized but talented chef. After all, *my* mom was. She made bread daily, not the kind that smelled and rose with yeast or was made in the oven or some sort of maker. No, she hand-measured her flour, baking powder, and warm water that she kneaded by hand. Her trusty cast iron pan was her baker. Much later, when we moved frequently, I saw her pan wrapped in newspaper or dish linens. If she were ever to leave overnight, I bet that pan would sit in the bottom of her footlocker under her clothes and shoes.

Erratic bus service and a job loss at Campbell's Soup prompted our move from Bell to El Monte. Our new apartment had four family residences, two on the bottom and two on the second floor. I know my parents chose this place because Park View Elementary was a block away, and Elliott Avenue had a bus line. An extra benefit was Mountain View Park—right across the street. Both ruled my world. School and play. Playing at school. The Navajo word for school is based on counting, *olta*. The word for playing is *naahne*. No connection whatsoever, but they were synonymous to me. Clay that smelled oily and got stuck under my fingernails. A play house with doors that opened and shut. Water-coloring on an easel, wearing a large old shirt as my smock. Blocks, Lincoln Logs, and Legos. Singing songs, exercising, and my God, the best of all, the playground. At some point we all took naps or rested quietly on a towel we brought from home.

My mother would have sent me to nap time with our best towel. Never having been formally educated, education was all-important to her. Dressed in heels and a sleeveless dress with her neat bouffant, my mom took our daily excursion to school seriously. Dressing up signaled nothing less than a holy excursion. She recalled the details of her older and younger siblings leaving home for boarding schools on a wagon or truck. She had envied them, unaware of the shameful stories connected to those schools. The days her brothers and sisters returned at breaks or at the end of the year were akin to holidays, so my school attendance generated pride. Even my brother wore button down shirts with pant hems our mom shortened or lengthened as needed. She cautioned me to listen to my teacher and play nicely, and she promised to be in a specific spot at the end of the day. For the most part, I did as I was told. My greatest fear was being kept from play.

Sometimes we walked to school with my best friend Becky, who lived in the second floor apartment next door. Becky had black hair, blue eyes, and freckles. She smiled easily and was always happy to see me. I have no idea how we became friends. My dad said by this time I knew some Spanish words and phrases. Maybe so. He might have given me undeserved credit, or been proud of how easily we had acclimated to our new El Monte neighborhood. Spanish is a beautiful language, and when I hear it, it still washes over me like warm water. Perhaps because we spoke Navajo and Becky's family spoke Spanish, our two languages felt like an equal sign—more proof of our best-friendship. At any rate, the two of us stumbled through English with one another when we were together, gradually gaining confidence and fluency.

In school, Becky and I were inseparable. We played house, Legos, Lincoln Logs, skipped holding hands, and lined up together. When we had to lie down, our teacher, a woman I recall as almost impossibly good-natured, played soft music as we lay on our towels-as-mats. My God she was patient with us. There might have been tussles and minor squabbles, but I behaved as my parents had instructed me, for school was heaven.

Becky and I weren't perfect, however. We found an unhealthy pleasure as the class panty inspectors. Thanks to the short dresses of 70s fashion, we had no trouble with our clean panty patrol. I'm certain it was me who invented this mean-spirited game, because Becky was generous and kind. She represented our better half. I might have alighted upon the pastime precisely because I wasn't overly scrupulous about this important brand of tidiness. In our defense, Becky and I never spoke or accused aloud, and we certainly never mentioned it after nap times. We were harmless in that respect. And thank goodness we never had to explain our unnatural panty surveillance. I'm sure we knew we were treading in naughty territory. Imagine the deep smiling sigh of pure contentment that I released when we retired from our inspections.

Recess, in contrast, operated under different, less surreptitious rules. Becky and I hurried to stand near the front of the line, or when I heard Becky call my name, I scrambled to join her. Social justice must have played a part in our line etiquette decisions, because if I got in line farther back, Becky joined me, or vice versa. As we made our exit from the classroom in orderly fashion, before we were allowed to break out in a run, she and I agreed what we would do: swings, teeter totter, monkey bars, or jumping ropes.

We both loved the free-standing teeter totter. This fought-over contraption was a large half circle made from metal pipes that seemed to pitch each child dangerously high into the sky; however, recently when I saw the original teeter totters that we had used, they appeared harmlessly small and safe. The exception was when the portable teeter-totter's base shifted a fraction during use. One day during recess, I was poised at the head of the line awaiting my turn, and as our anticipation grew, my peers pushed. I steadied myself, but I stepped too close to the base. Consequently, the tips of my toes were crushed under an onslaught of metal. What awful hot pain. I refused to cry out because I was next in line. I finally got on the coveted see-saw and smiled through my agony, limping back to class when our teacher rang her hand bell. I hadn't learned of deep pain yet, but this is the first I remember of bearing through even a small physical trauma. I later studied my bruised toes during my bath, not telling my parents for fear I would have to stay home. Becky never noticed, nor did my teacher or parents. But in the quiet solitude of my bed that evening, I found a position where the bedding wouldn't touch my injury.

I wasn't the only one to suffer a mishap to an extremity. My brother Dean lost his thumb nail when my mom stepped on it with her stiletto heel. She said she never heard a peep from him, no sound at all. She hadn't caught her misstep until she felt the imbalance of her heel. When she checked, she found a small fingernail attached to the point of her heel. Today Dean has a fantastically thick thumbnail. Moreover I realize now he was far braver than I was, proven by the fact that he was younger and didn't cry. I, on the other hand, might have cried loudly, but I didn't want to lose my place in line.

Before-school activities, unlike school itself, were pure torture. I stood still as my mom brushed, then sectioned off my hair with a comb, then braided it tugging and pulling it into place. If I resisted her, she reined me in tighter. Better to get it over with, I thought, and I endured my brief confinement by listening to radio stations that played a lot of Credence Clearwater Revival and The Beatles and ballads on Top 40. The songs eased me through my mother's maltreatment. At some point during these awful sessions, I decided that when I was older, I would never brush my hair again. A convenient solution for a child whose mom did everything for her. My mom took care of us, feeding, dressing, and escorting us to and from school, sanctioning our play, preparing dinner and getting us to bed. The days were uneventful and in their uneventfulness blissful, mainly because my mom championed us. When I recall these times, they feel vacation-y, complete with perfect Southern California weather.

Our apartment had two bedrooms. My brother and I shared a room. It probably was a small room, but when I went to bed, my brother seemed far away across a great expanse.

I sometimes stared at the closet door, and I always made sure the sliding door was entirely shut. My dad said sometimes my brother and I camped out in the living room because we were frightened by an elusive bat man. Was that his wispy image that floated into our room through the window? Was it the family directly beneath us who raised a ruckus that disturbed our sleep? Sometimes we heard a banging on our floor, signaling my brother and me to halt in mid-run. When I saw these neighbors outside in front of the apartment, I stayed upstairs until they drove away or returned to their apartment. I was struck by the long unkempt blond hair on the man, the woman, and the children. They made disapproving loud sounds, though I'm sure *our* sounds ricocheted in their direction far too many times to count.

One incident stands out to reinforce the crucial importance of school to me. I had come across from the park to get a snack or water at the apartment when I saw the long blond-haired man from downstairs in his car. He looked surly or bad-tempered. As I made my way around his car, he called out, *Hey. Hey little girl.*

I clearly knew that was me. When I paused, I noticed his car was idling. Alone, he parked towards the driveway leading out to Maxson Road. Before he called out, I saw his face, and when he saw me see him, he brightened up. I'm sure I had observed other instant transformations before, but I knew that his wasn't genuine. He smiled and that's when he inched the car closer to me.

Hey. Your mama asked me to get you a bike.

The word *bike* got my attention, and I gave my fullest attention to this semi-stranger. His blond hair glistened and some hair near his face and scalp was pooled in oily clusters. I could see the individual strands in his beard. His angry blue eyes shimmered. I saw the furrowed brows, like he wasn't used to smiling and showing his teeth. There was a greasy quality in his shirtless state.

That's right. Your mama said she wants me to buy you a bike.

There was that magical word again. I took a half step closer to him because I was under the spell of a single word. If I hadn't heard the word *bike*, I would have kept moving. But now I imagined racks of bikes, shiny blues and reds, like those I had seen in Montgomery Ward.

Just then all sound was altered. Like symphony music rising within me, a film we watched in school just days before rose before me. *Stranger Danger*. A police officer visited our class and shared how a stranger could lure a child into unsafe places using candy, toys, and sometimes threats. As I listened to the uniformed policeman, I imagined that if I were abducted, I would never see my mother again. Of that I was sure, and that conviction planted me squarely back on the sidewalk where I stood.

Hey.

The stringy-haired blond man broke the spell, and when I shifted my attention back to him, he was no longer smiling. The furrows had deepened and his face was lowered just enough for me to see an expression that matched what I thought was his true face.

C'mon. Get in.

The *Get in* made a grating sound. He opened his driver door as he started moving in my direction.

That's when I heard my teacher's clear voice intoning *Stranger Danger* and felt an internal shove that forced me into a run that could easily have sent me sprawling. Instead, I felt as if some force had lifted and propelled me into the speed of a run, where my feet barely glanced the ground. I raced, veering far from the man's possible reach. I still marvel at the speed with which I flew up the stairs and threw myself into the apartment so loudly that my mom turned from whatever she was doing to immediately question me.

Where's your brother? Nitsili shai?

I cried a lie. *I can't find him.*

For all I knew, that man from downstairs in the car had my brother. My mom stopped what she was doing to hurry out the door. Though she told me to stay in place, I couldn't. First I recognized my narrow miss with Strange Danger, then I imagined Dean disappearing into the car, balancing the awful equation. And a more harrowing thought, I could lose my mother along with Dean, or instead of him. How imaginative fear can be. I was in tears by then. I stayed at my mother's heels as she clicked and clacked down the stairs, but I saw the car was gone, and little Dean was climbing the stairs, smiling at our sudden greeting to his arrival, as if we waited for his return in this fine manner. So that was how different our lives were.

19

Lessons linger and sometimes resurface in odd times, but the Stranger Danger episode stayed with me. I had stepped right up to death's door, and before I could knock, I had been transported back to the safety of my life. This vulnerability was a cold call, and I had to make a new place for it in my thinking.

This might have been the first time I felt true fear. Adults could lie. Adults could be dangerous. Lives could change course in seconds. The fear that I had formerly associated with the dark abruptly flipped, and I saw with certainty that terrible events could happen during the day under sunny skies.

Needless to say, my trust in my teacher deepened. I don't know if I told my mother, but as tall as she looked to me, I knew that man downstairs was taller and stronger. He also possessed a car, a vehicle that could crush me, follow and run me down, and take me away from my family. This instantly reduced the living, breathing weight of my life to powerlessness.

From then on, I no longer ran freely around the apartment complex. I never ever wanted to see that man's face or hear his voice again. I certainly never saw that car again. In time, a new man parked his car where the blue car had been. Stranger Danger let me see that someone near us could harm us.

Another outcome of this narrow escape was that I kept a closer eye on my brother. He already stayed near me in the park, having heard from our mom about my responsibility as his sister. I allowed him some choices, slides or swings, and luckily, he minded me. Interconnectedness now made a lot of sense. I heard my mom's constant admonitions to take care of my brother as *baa aholya*, but another command was *adahwiilya*. Sometimes Navajo visitors to our home would say this before stepping over the threshold to the great outer world. It means to protect and watch over one another. Since my escape, this command on the importance of community rang within me with the force of a powerfully struck bell.

Armed with this new insight, I got up earlier than usual to see my dad off to work. I hadn't thought about how much we depended on his return. I watched as he tied the laces of his black steel-toed boots. After he double knotted them, he stood up and reached for his metal lunchbox, leaving me with, B*ye*, as he shut the door.

That day, I decided that I wanted to learn how to tie my shoelaces. If I learned this, I reasoned, my mom and dad wouldn't have to tie them for me. I would be that much less of an inconvenience. Thus Becky found me sitting on the top step of the staircase. Like me, she wore Keds with circular rubber toe boxes with laced shoestrings. She sat beside me as she looked at my twists and loops. I came to the same impasse, tangled knots.

Realizing that we needed help, Becky said, *Let me get my sister*, and she hurried home. In a minute, her sister showed up and modeled the process on Becky's shoe. When we couldn't manage her first method, she showed us the bunny-ears method. Two knotted bunny ears. We practiced with one shoe in our laps, then Becky's sister told us to tie one another's shoe. As I tied Becky's shoe, the sounds of traffic and children receded, and I could almost hear my heart beat as I concentrated, making the required loops and turns. I knew I had gotten it right when background noise returned. *Cool*, Becky's sister said as she stood up and walked back to their apartment. By lunch time, Becky and I raced one another to tie our laces, counting aloud as we did. This achievement was made real by the fact that my parents practiced it daily. I hadn't quite connected the colors, shapes, and words I learned in school to the life of my parents, but shoelace tying was a real skill that they performed. My world felt large, and my best friend knew this skill, too. What liberation.

Another liberation, quite different but just as real, were the multiple volumes of brown leather-like bound books that my parents bought. Some families get an encyclopedia set, but my parents ordered Bible stories from Old and New Testaments with colorful illustrations. I couldn't read, but I flipped from one illustration to the next wondering what the pictures meant. Since only one of us could read in our household, the responsibility fell on my dad. He read one section from a volume each night. Before reading, he always said in Navajo, *Listen carefully so you can remember.*

He read in English, but then translated to Navajo as my mom listened from the kitchen. My dad lay on his stomach as he read, and my brother and I scooted close to him. Seeing our dad read and explain to us the stories from a printed book elevated him to new heights in our eyes, and somehow we were able to hang onto him as he soared. This was better than TV-land. When he read and translated from English to

Navajo, I felt an inexplicable safety that protected us within an unseen hogan, like a great dome.

As my dad read to us, I felt that a greatness sustained me, one that had formed after my narrow escape from the man in the car. Even though I knew what cold vulnerability could look like, I felt sheltered when my family was together listening to the Bible stories. Some made sense, and some didn't. Nonetheless, when I came home from school, I opened the book to review the pictures that my dad had read about, and then I previewed the new set of pictures for our next reading. Since my dad read to us, and since I listened as he said we should, and since I read along with the movement of his index finger, I truly thought I was reading.

Living in El Monte was a long vacation compared with what was to follow. We lived across the street from a park, down the street from my school, and if we walked in the opposite direction, as we did many times with our mom, we came to a small market. There she bought sardines that she scooped into folds of newsprint, and there we also received three small dishes of vanilla ice cream. This was my favorite lunch before going to half day school in the afternoon. My mom fried the sardines in corn meal. I picked the skin and meat off with my fingers to scoop the bits into my mouth. Messy but delicious. This warm silvery and cold creamy white meal was heaven.

My dad was a certified welder by then. He worked full-time and caught a series of public buses to reach his worksite. His steady employment oiled and operated our lives. While we lived comfortably, a life that my parents were proud of, they had little savings to ride through his job loss when it abruptly arrived. We lived on their meager savings, but when that ran out, we had no choice but to move. My mom packed her pan, our clothes, and the Bible story set. We left behind our couch, dining set, beds, chests of drawers, and a bookshelf. My dad walked over to tell Becky's dad he could have the furniture but to move it out as soon as possible. We packed everything that my parents wanted to take, a few boxes that they placed into a Yellow Cab that arrived in the evening. I cried. I saw Becky and her family when they came to say goodbye. I didn't hold Becky long in our embrace because she reminded me of what I was leaving. Before we parted, I thrust my doll into her arms. I cherished my doll and Becky, so it seemed right that they should be together. The lights and people blurred and streaked through my tears as we huddled in the cab and made our way to the bus station.

Much later, I asked my dad about why we moved from El Monte, and he blamed my maternal grandfather Ray Begay. Even after a half century, my dad believes his father-in-law was behind his job loss. He didn't know about unemployment help or other social safeguards that could have kept us in this place he loved. My dad never cared for his in-laws. He quietly called my *Cheii* a wizard.

CHAPTER 2

First Grade: The White House

Before we moved to Oakland, my dad and his brother Kee New Begody built a one-room house. The exterior was tar paper, the floor and walls were pine, and we had a wood-burning half-metal barrel stove. The house had a bed for my parents, a built-in closet, and a hand-made wooden table. It had open shelves for dishes, food, books, and a manual record player. Dean and I slept on a twin mattress that my mother stored in the closet.

We moved to this cozy house when we returned from California. Our home had no electricity or modern conveniences, but the door faced east, a holy direction, and the windows faced west and north. My dad painted the trim green.

We returned to our extended family. In this area, nestled in a small valley with an ancient air, surrounded by junipers, we called *gad*, we returned from our El Monte vacation. My paternal grandmother, *Nali*, was the matriarch. My *nali* lived in a hogan. Her daughter Sadie and her husband Kee Nez Begay, my favorite uncle, had seven children. They lived half a mile south of us in a bigger version of a house like ours, also constructed by the labors of strong-handed relatives. Kee

Nez was my mom's oldest brother and Sadie was my dad's older sister. We visited them often and I was close to their children Venne, Dan, and Marilyn whom I called my brothers and sisters. Their clans were the same as mine but in reverse.

My *nali*'s mother, my great grandmother, S*hinalii Sani* Lola Billy, lived separately in a hogan 300 yards west of us. She lived next to her son Guy Billy, and his wife, who we called Jessie *Bima*, and their three children. S*hinalii Sani* was my oldest living relative, and I loved her dearly. She and I took long walks to satisfy an invisible itch of hers. We walked to faraway cedar trees, *gad*, and sat under their shade while she studied the landscape. I stared, wanting to see what she saw. Sometimes she told me what the area looked like when her family first settled there. And she told me about people I would never meet because they had passed away. I was her only audience when she shared old narratives from before my birth. When she was ready to walk home, I accompanied her. Inside her hogan, she searched for her ready-to-eat snacks: saltine crackers, miniature boxes of cereal, and a can of soda pop. Hearing the can tab pulled open followed by the fizz of carbonation takes me back to S*hinalii Sani*. Sometimes she had Fig Newtons, which I still refer to as grandma cookies. Because no one locked their doors in our area, she hid her snacks. Sometimes they were in an inconspicuous bucket by the door where she kept her kindling, other times under her bedroll. She didn't have a bed in her home. In fact, there wasn't a stitch of furniture besides the cupboard, her loom, and a wood burning stove.

Shinalii Sani's cupboard held her dishes, cooking ware, and some food. To seal off the cupboard's insides, she sewed a simple small curtain made from green broadcloth. She used a string to hold the curtain, hammering a nail at each end where she tied the lines of the string. When I first saw this, I made up an excuse to drink water from a ladle in her water pail that she covered with a cloth. I peeked behind the curtain, which revealed commodity goods and sometimes a canister of salt and baking powder. No matter how many times I saw it, the curtain hinted at mystery to me.

Shinalii Sani slept on a bedroll and sat on the floor to weave and eat and pass the day. From her sitting-on-the-floor position, her folded knees with her feet tucked under her, she would raise herself up with her hands, knuckles to the ground. Because she wore the traditional gathered skirt, her movement from sitting to standing was fluid. I recall the light catching on the gathered pleats, creating a ripple effect. What strong hamstrings and upper body strength she possessed until she passed at 103. After our snacks were eaten, she folded her loose crumbs into her outer gathered skirt and sprinkled them well away from her home. Then she returned to her weaving. Here again, she sat on her knees and feet, her unsupported back straight but flexible enough to make the movements necessary for weaving. Hers was a comfortable pose. She wove until her sight diminished. Her rugs were small to medium-sized, all wool dyed from local plants. She didn't sell many to the trading post, but relatives bought them from her. I saw her rugs used as chair or seat coverings. My mom owned a few.

Shinalii Sani's other daughter, my paternal grandmother's sister, and her husband, lived east of us. I called her Teen *Bi Masani*. Teen was her grandson, but his maternal grandparents were raising him. He was seven days younger than I was. We never said Teen's grandfather's name. We rarely saw him at home, and when we visited, he disappeared. No one asked about him. This made me think he was a ghost. I only heard his voice once. He was a medicine man who could be seen carrying his knapsack as he walked to the sheep corral or to repair fencing or other odds and ends. He wore a traditional Navajo bun that we called *atsiiyel*, and he wore moccasins that he likely made for himself, his wife, and Teen. They were a quiet family. Soon after returning to Gap, I became reacquainted with my cousins. Other relatives visited and welcomed us home from the trauma of living in *bilagaanah tah*.

When my mom, Dean, and I visited my favorite grandmother, *Shima Sani* Lucy, my dad stayed away, as tradition prohibits sons-in-law from interacting with mothers-in-law, but my dad also harbored suspicion of his in-laws. I hadn't heard the stories and gossip about my dear maternal grandparents yet, but when I did, I remained fiercely loyal to my *Ma Sani*. In line with cultural tradition, my maternal grandmother never spoke my dad's name, instead asking about *alchini bizhe'e*, the children's father. Completely correct and polite. I always saw my grandmother as a tower of kindness and manners, someone who never lost her sense of calm evenhandedness. She never rolled her eyes as my paternal grandmother did, and I never recall her judging anyone. She laughed at all my look-at-me antics, and her touch on my crown or smoothing down of my nesty hair always made me feel safe.

Of course, I didn't know the earlier version of these grandparents, the brewers of moonshine, the cursers and the brawlers. Their alcoholism drove my mom away. One older brother had threatened to skin her alive and kill me. He was a tall, forceful man who didn't mind hitting his wife in public, and my mom didn't want to test his angry promise. Pregnant with my brother Dean, she resolved to run away. One morning, she let out the sheep, made a breakfast of naan-like bread and coffee, and instead of sheepherding, she swaddled me in a cradleboard and packed her small bundle of clothes to walk to the home of her oldest brother, Kee Nez Begay. Only when the sheep didn't return did my grandparents learn my mom had left. It was some time before my mom ventured to visit her parents again.

Perhaps my dad called my *cheii* a wizard because my maternal grandmother had been a hand trembler. Or maybe his suspicion stemmed simply from our great love of my *Shima Sani*. Some today might describe hand trembling as an ancient art of information-gathering or an unmentionable art form. *Shima Sani* interpreted answers communicated from a void that made her hand shake and dance. Her right index finger was broken and never reset. I knew her by this finger, which she used freely despite its fragile, painful appearance. I winced whenever she carried a butcher knife, newly sharpened against a stone to cut a crying sheep's jugular.

During the time we were away in California, my maternal grandmother was baptized. I don't know if my *cheii* was saved, but he didn't make his popular moonshine anymore. When I met my grandmother again, she went to church, smiled to no end when she saw us, and butchered a sheep to celebrate our family's return. That's the grandmother I knew. I shadowed her and did whatever chores I could to be with her. She was a light that I couldn't get enough of.

She renounced hand trembling once she was baptized into Christianity. She identified herself as an *yoodlaanii*, literally translated as a believer. A Christian. How much my grandmother practiced her new faith was unclear. She was kind, helpful, and loving, but she went to church only occasionally. I never heard her sing a hymn the way I heard my *Nali* and Aunt Sadie, nor did she read her Navajo Bible. The Baptist church she attended was led initially by her younger brother-in-law Lee Begay. Her third son Jerry Begay eventually became its minister. Once I sat beside her in the Baptist church, half listening. Neither of us sang the Navajo hymns. When the service was over, she rose and I followed. Sitting down for what seemed like several hours too many might have taxed her beyond endurance. She was an active person who sat still only when she ate at the end of her day.

Soon she stopped attending church altogether, although she never reverted to her earlier behavior. All I understood was how kind and true my maternal grandmother was. She never held back her approval and love of me. I imagine it was in part because my brother and I spoke Navajo, unlike some of her other grandchildren. She was wiry and active. She saddled and rode horseback daily. All her clothes were made by hand. This included a long-sleeved velveteen blouse with a hidden pocket on center where she fastened a turquoise brooch. The cuffs of her sleeves were lined in calico or printed material that she rolled up when she butchered a sheep. She also wore a turquoise bracelet. When she was going to the trading post, she put on a double strand of beaded turquoise.

When we returned home from California, my mom began making her mother's clothes. Whether she had made them before we left for California I can't say. I do recall *Shima Sani* saying to her daughter, *Only you make them fit me so well*. This compliment from *Shima Sani* quickened my mom's industry. When my grandmother gave my mom fabric for a dress or a shirt, my mom's measuring tape was a string that she marked with a pen or pencil. She used the same string to measure her mother's waist and length and her shoulder span and arms. Anyone else might question the meaning of each mark along the string, but my mom knew which was which. If no string was available, she measured with her hands and the span between her thumb and little finger. She used the same method to measure the geometric designs on her rugs. I examined my hands after observing my mother use hers as her tool. I knew my hands held unknown mysteries and that I would use them for all my days as the adults in my life had used theirs.

I never saw my mom wear the clothes she had worn in California. Now she changed back into her traditional handmade shirt and gathered skirt. Her heels disappeared. She wore canvas shoes with white crew socks. However, she kept her hair in a bouffant.

My parents signed up for government assistance to get commodity food, but because we didn't have a vehicle, we often made do, stranded in this beautiful land with cedars, dried stream beds with ancient shells, sand bars that made excellent tumbling mats, and sandstone rocks, all under the great cornflower blue sky. My dad couldn't find work in our rural setting. He might have gotten a job in Utah, where my Uncle Kee Nez Begay worked in a sawmill, but my dad didn't like his brother-in-law. Faced with no means to support us, he began to leave home for days at a time. He drank to escape, and he escaped to the comforting arms of other women. Telephones didn't exist here, but word traveled fast. It wasn't very long after our return that when I heard the name Fred, I knew people were gossiping about my dad.

To support our family, my mom returned to weaving rugs, a skill she had learned early. As a youth she watched her mom weave gigantic rugs that my *cheii* and my mom's brothers adjusted the great loom. I see a little version of my mom observing and storing these in her weaving heart for the later visual stories she will weave, and so she did, to feed us. She wove large rugs, but not as large as her first teacher's, using the wool her mother or her mother-in-law gave her.

My mom carded the wool by hand using wooden hand tools with short metal bristles. She placed a tarp in her lap and as she raked the wool to puffs, debris fell from the carding tools. I imagined that the sound of the metal bristles raking against one another was like the sound of a giant's hair being combed. My job was to shake the tarp and spread it on her lap once she resumed. Off to the side, she piled up puffy wool fluffs that she spun using another hand tool, a drop spindle whorl made from a cedar. She placed a wooden circular divider to catch the spun wool. I loved the spinning sound. I hadn't yet seen a ballerina or ice skater twirl, but years later, when I saw one for the first time, I thought of my mother's drop spindle whorl. It made a happy dancing sound, and I knew this meant the washing and dying were next.

My mother unwound the spun wool into loose woolen ropes. She produced natural dyes by boiling local plants she had collected, although she sometimes bought special colors from the trading post. Dyeing meant building an open fire and heating water in a big pail to wash the white wool she planned to use. She used the same procedure for the dye-added water, selecting a long stick to move the wool inside the metal bucket. This was a truly magical caldron as I witnessed the white wool transform into another color. If my mom did this in cold weather, it was pleasant to sit nearby for warmth. Afterwards, she let the water cool then wrung the woolen bundles clean, drying them on the same tarp she had used earlier. It was a one-person task, but it was work. My mom's fingers were dry and cracked. Her nails were brittle. No amount of hand cream relieved her dry fingertips.

When she had enough balls of yarn, she began making the warp, a thin string refined by hand that would be attached vertically to the loom. This procedure was tedious: my mom sat on the ground rolling each woolen strand thinner and tighter, pausing to count and straighten the warp. She continually checked the tension by strumming it with her fingertips. A mistake here could result in an asymmetrical rug. She was a study in patience. Later when she sped up her rug weaving, she purchased a big woolen spool of warp string from the trading post.

After she tied the upper and lower warp to rods and onto the loom with a thick rope, she set up her wooden loom under a great cedar tree that we called a shade house. I spent many happy hours playing with toys near my mom as she wove. The beating of the weaving fork is a soft but heavy sound, one that reminds me of my mother's hand patting my back to settle me to sleep.

That summer I stopped wearing shoes when I outgrew them. I wore a dress but ran about barefooted. Since this neared a riverbed, this area had a smattering of smooth, sun-heated pebbles. I learned the dance of flitting from one cool spot or sliver of shade to another in the searing heat. As a last resort, I used my heels to skip through the hot sand. Often, skipping and prancing, I made it all the way to my paternal grandmother's. The closer I came to her home, the faster I raced, for her hogan was in a bare, dirt-packed, treeless stretch of land. Only when I started school in September did my mom buy me a new pair of shoes.

My mother wove from morning to night, stopping only to prepare meals for us, clean the dishes, and sweep. Then she resumed weaving. When she neared the very end of a rug, my Aunt Sadie, also a weaver, would visit often. Finally, my mom would remove the rug, brush and iron it. Sometimes she let my Auntie Sadie sell her rug. Whatever they agreed upon, it was a quiet affair, and my mom seemed satisfied with the food and money my aunt brought in return. When my mom made the trip to make the sale at the trading post herself, we had a large entourage: most of my aunt's seven children, my paternal grandmother, my brother and me, along with my Aunt Sadie and sometimes my Uncle Kee Nez. The ride to Gap Trading Post meant food, laundry, and gasoline. It felt like a carnival ride with a trail of rising dust, thanks to my aunt's love of speed and my encouraging cry of *Yeego!*

I stood near my mom as she waited to present her rug to the trading post manager. Standing next to her, I finally stopped using her gathered skirt as my wrap after many slaps to my head and being told, *Stop*, finally learning to stand still and observe. My mom had wrapped her rug in a clean and ironed Blue Bird flour sack. She unfolded the bleached white material to reveal her newest creation. The manager squinted closely as he checked the weft to determine the tightness of her weave. He also studied her two grey hills design while he made approving nods and sounds. *Nizhoni.* He complimented her, and then gave her the transaction terms divided in three ways: food, cash, and credit. My mom bought basics: flour, baking powder, cans of peaches, Spam, onions, potatoes, and fruit, usually apples. I watched her giving my aunt gas money, and very occasionally handing an older cousin money to buy ice cream for us, the children, from the nearby burger joint. My mom had learned that if she wanted to buy her children ice cream, she needed to buy it for her brother's children as well. Most often, she bought a can or two of soda pop or a candy bar that we all shared later in the hush and fading light of our small home, sly snacks after we were all alone. The rest of the rug payment was recorded on a credit slip kept by the trading post manager, which my mom used to buy groceries at the trading post until she finished another rug.

As the sole provider, my mother now occupied the role my dad had enjoyed when we lived in Oakland. This loss of station gradually shamed him into violence. When he returned home from his latest girlfriend's, he bickered with my mom quietly, but over time the bickering turned into fights. Navajo words for arguing describe having *too many hard words*, implying pointless arguing. Another meaning is *to agitate or hit another person with words*, like a battering. My parents often waited to argue until my brother and I went outside to play. My dad would call my mom names. Occasionally she was able to sidestep his provocation by weaving. No doubt he sometimes attacked her physically. However, my dad wasn't much taller than my mom, and in my mom he challenged a woman who wouldn't shy away from calling on her muscle gods. She helped haul water and chopped wood.

She also helped with cattle and sheep. She still rode horseback. My father wouldn't get beyond a few punches given my mom's ability to fist back. She sometimes pinned him until he gave up. She said she never beat him more than he did her. More than once she chased him away with a whirling rope or batting stick, but they never used the axe, knives, or firearms—common items in our household. My mom only used her bent barrel rifle for small game hunting.

My parents obviously followed unspoken brawling rules, and other considerations tempered their actions as well. My dad may have been afraid of my mom's brothers. They were tall, and they drank and fought. My dad wouldn't have survived their onslaught. My mean uncle had threatened my mom before, but I'm sure he wouldn't have minded teaching my dad a lesson or two. My aunts were a handful—strong, young, and unafraid of physical risks. Needless-to-say, my dad was careful, convinced by his stature to refrain from public displays of anger. The exception was when he had home-court advantage.

After leaving her own home, my mom lived among my dad's relatives. Her mother-in-law was a gossip, happiest talking about others. The descriptive sentence in Navajo roughly translated is *Gossip tastes best to her*. A periodic, welcome visitor was my mom's older brother, who labored five days a week in a sawmill in Utah. When he drove from Fredonia or Kanab to his home near ours, he arrived late, slept, then did chores Saturday and part of Sunday before returning to Utah. Occasionally he took time on the weekends to visit my mom. I recall my mom lost her voice and had to hold her aching side from their laughter. I recall how my mom standing by his truck window as they shared old stories, lapsing into side-splitting laughter. He might have meant to stop briefly, but when he and his younger sister, share stories of the past, they lost track of time. Perhaps it was watching their interaction that made me love this uncle. Much, much later, my older daughter described Kee Nez having Buddha's smile and kindness. On Sunday mornings, when my uncle's family went to worship at the Baptist church, he and my paternal uncle, Guy Billy, held a sweat lodge. My dad sometimes joined them. While my uncle worked far from home, he used traditional cleaning to harmonize himself before returning to Utah.

Only once did I see my parents battle openly. I had entered the house for a drink of water when I saw that my mom had pinned my dad on the bed. Both panted and cursed one another beneath their ragged breathing, using words I didn't understand or hadn't ever heard my parents say. When they saw me, they pretended to laugh, but they didn't fool me. I stood aghast, trying to comprehend this new sight.

My dad said, *Lebby, help me. Get that gun for me.*

I turned to see a revolver on the floor. All my relatives used guns. The exception was my paternal grandmother, but my *Ma Sani* Lucy had one to shoot at coyotes when she was herding sheep. I had seen my *cheii* clean his revolver and rifle. My aunts, my mom's sisters, had them too.

Shoot your mom.

Mesmerized I reached for the gun, but then my mom said, *Shoot your dad, Shiyahzi.*

She uttered the command in Navajo, adding the endearment *Shiyazhi*. Dear or darling. I was too young to see any irony in this.

I touched the gun and felt its weight when I picked it up. I put it down because both parents looked at me with terrible expectations.

I'm telling my Nali, I blurted, as I escaped and raced to her hogan. I believed my dad's mother would put a stop to this havoc.

When I entered her hogan, I stammered in a rush of words between hiccups and sobs. In the space of minutes, I had developed a distressing stutter that took me years to get rid of. I expected my *Nali* to take immediate action to restore order. Instead she sat up from her prone position to grill me. *How long have they been fighting? Have they fought like this before? How did your mother look?*

I decided that rather than answer my *nali*, I'd go find my Great-Uncle Guy Billy, who would be able to separate my parents. It was surely just a matter of time before one of my parents reached for the revolver next to the bed. Any minute I expected the ping and echo of gunfire. But before I reached the door, my grandmother sprang up, grabbed me and held me tight. Evidently children must be separated when they squabbled or fought, but adults were allowed to operate by a different set of rules.

I cried in frustration and fear, recalling that my dad's father had died when my dad was just a toddler. My father grew up listening to stories about his dad, a person he only knew in his dreams. I had no doubt that I would grow up the same way. My *nali* held me, and only after an hour or so passed did she let me go, allowing Dean and me to walk what seemed a terribly long vexing path. I worried about what we would find, but I remained silent about what I had witnessed because I didn't want to upset my brother. These and more confused thoughts and feelings churned in me as my brother and I headed home in the fading afternoon light. I don't think I have ever walked as slowly as I did that day.

I learned later that even though my *nali* had quickly become aware of all that was taking place, she would not intervene. She might have seen this as a private marital squabble, but I saw it, because of the gun, as much more. It revealed to me that behind a heavy curtain existed secrets not only between my parents but among my other relatives as well. I was just now permitted a glimpse of what others had long known and continued to harbor in silence.

When my brother and I arrived that early evening, my mom was hanging our freshly hand-laundered clothes to dry, and our dinner was still warm in the covered pan. My dad sat on the bed where they had fought earlier, reading an old paper. Neither of my parents ever brought up their strange requests that I hurt the other. I was dazed and bewildered that they could remain silent in the aftermath of their senseless, criminal appeals. Though I still loved them unreservedly with a child's love, something had inexplicably changed. My world felt off, slightly askew, for months after this. If anything upsetting happened, anything out of the ordinary, I decided it was part of the way things really were along this new, no longer even plane. It was natural and normal that everyone I loved suffered.

Not long after this, my mom finished another rug, and along with groceries, she brought home new shoes with laces for me. She also washed all my dresses, ironed them, and packed them with my underwear and socks in a small blue suitcase. Then she woke me earlier than usual to bathe and shampoo my hair. Before my hair could completely dry, she braided it in two strands. Soon my Aunt Sadie arrived. My mom, brother and I climbed into her pickup and set off. We reached the junction where Gap Trading Post sits, but instead of stopping, my aunt steered left, heading south on Highway 89. We reached another junction, and we turned left again, this time east on Highway 160. I heard *olta* and *Tonaneesdizi* several times, but I didn't take the words to heart, even though the little blue suitcase with my clothes was stowed nearby. My brother and I observed the passing scenery. I suspect both of us entertained hopeful thoughts of ice cream, or the wonderful elusive hamburger that we had seen others eat but had never tasted ourselves.

To our left, great jagged cliff walls revealed successive epochs from long ago, while to the right mounds of grey briars stretched into the distance. If anyone hikes to the west through the briars, she will eventually halt at a canyon drop, where she will see the Colorado River patiently weaving its way through time.

In Tuba City, my aunt drove in the direction of the Dairy Queen, the trading post, and the hospital. But before we reached the hospital, she pulled into a parking lot where other pickups were parked. I saw families with children near my age. This didn't seem right at all. Both my aunt and mom were quiet now. The air became heavy and hot. I felt a sudden thirst. Only my brother looked around with a smile on his face.

The unsaid finally materialized when our mom told Dean to stay with my aunt, lifted the suitcase in one hand and grasped mine with her other. The two of us made our way towards a large building. We followed other families, and a girl ahead of us turned to look at me over her shoulder. I saw light shining on her wet cheek, but I still didn't make sense of it all. I had experienced a strange summer during which strange things took place between my parents, and I couldn't imagine life getting any more unfamiliar.

My mother began droning instructions in random order. *Listen to the teachers. Find people who can help you braid your hair. I will come for you on Fridays to check you out. I will wait for you here.*

Her voice was strained, reminding me of her entreaty that I shoot my dad. I tightened my grip on her hand and she squeezed back. We walked along the buckled sidewalk surrounded by thick cottonwood trees with leaves clattering like tiny drum beats above us.

Foregoing my usual whys and whens, my customary reactions to new experiences, I remained silent. Perhaps out of a sense of unreality and a child's trust, I decided to let things unfold on their own, the way flower petals unfurl under the warmth of the sun. If I had understood more, I would have urged my mother to make more promises, impossible promises. I certainly wouldn't have continued mutely along the path that led to the concrete building with locked metal doors where I heard keys jingle on belts and lanyards.

What is this place? I asked in Navajo.

Olta, she answered.

At this time, I was only familiar with my half-day classes and the pleasant walk with my mom to and from school. The large building didn't hold any peculiar significance. My vocabulary of school was limited and my understanding more limited still. I didn't know about tribal boarding schools.

When we entered the building, two tables divided several seated women from us. My mom took papers from a plastic bag inside her handbag. I listened to the conversation, but I soon lost interest, instead looking around. The walls were white painted cinder blocks. The ceiling was high, and I could hear the sounds bounce off the ceiling and walls, then back again. I huddled close to my mom's warmth while I turned to take in the entire cavernous room. Everything looked dull, nothing like my Park View Elementary. I saw a girl my age trail after one of the women who had been seated at the table. The girl's mother stayed on "our" side of the table. The girl turned to glance back at her mother, a woman dressed like my mom, who stared after her until her daughter was out of sight. That's when I became aware of sounds coming from where the girl had just disappeared. I heard a hum of voices; girl sounds now awakened my curiosity, and I decided they sounded happy and welcoming.

Later my mom said it took two staff workers to unlock my grip, not just my arms but my legs as well, from her. She said my eyes had a wildness that she saw in a mustang when she started breaking it the first day. She said my deep sounds came from somewhere deeper than my throat.

How long did it take for me to get over my mom's betrayal? Everything blurred and time broke. I have fragmented images of lining up to get a scoop of Vaseline from a large container that one of the dorm mothers dished out on a wooden spatula. We rubbed the translucent jelly on our arms, legs, and faces to walk out into the stiff breezes that felt like sand blasting. Tuba City winds. When we reached the cafeteria, we had sand on all oiled surfaces. When I licked my lips, I could feel granules of sand, so my first few breakfast bites included grit with my toast and oatmeal. I don't recall anything about my classroom or my teacher, just the intensity when Friday came, of waiting for my mom to check me out as she had promised.

All day, I listened for my name to be called. I imagined my mother on the road from home, and when I visualized where she should be in Tuba City, I granted her some permitted delays like a gasoline stop or a grocery stop or possibly a rug-selling stop. I even allowed her a few extra minutes of travel time to buy me an ice cream, never mind the impracticality of this. After all, my mom had worn ridiculous stilettos carrying my brother and had asked me to shoot my dad, so buying me an ice cream was not all that far-fetched.

When she finally arrived, I torpedoed out and found my mom standing in the waiting room. The mere sight of her heightened my senses. She appeared perfectly, almost dreamily arranged in her glory. It wasn't just her puffed up hair, or even the trace of lip color. She was there for me. I didn't see any ice cream, but that was fine. She half-carried me as I glued myself to her warmth and scent. We floated our happy way to my Aunt Sadie and Dean.

My aunt smiled and said, *Thank you for joining us. We waited all day for you.* Although she had seven children, she hadn't lost her sense of humor nor her generous, ready smile. My paternal grandmother sat in the middle, so my brother and I stood in the cab of the truck and held our mom's knees to steady ourselves as my aunt peeled out of the school parking lot. I loved it when she sped down hills and around curves. I yelled, *Naani!*

If our reunion was a heaven, our return on Sunday was the torturous opposite. I fought all the way. I refused to have my hair washed or brushed or to get dressed. I taxed my mom's usual calm demeanor. I had to be carried into the truck. My mom consoled me by holding me in her lap. My aunt offered me a stick of gum, which I chewed as my salty tears mixed with sweet peppermint. When we reached the junction, my aunt made a quick purchase of two cans of soda from the gas station shop. She offered me a can to pacify me, but my tears spilled over again once I saw the highway.

No amount of sweet bribery worked. If I was a wild mustang before, I was a wolverine now. I bared my teeth to claw and hide. I may have growled, but I definitely acquired the skill of hovering close to the ground as a quickly learned defense to avoid returning to boarding school. At one point, I hid under the truck. Only when my mom walked away did I crawl out, and before I could drop on all fours again, my Aunt Sadie caught and held me in a fierce grip. They carried and wrestled me back into the building.

My mom's face stiffened and appeared void of expression. She gave me one touch on my head as she whispered softly to me, more for her heart than mine. Two more dorm staff held me as my mom and aunt hurried out.

My mom checked me out only one more time, when I left there for good. Until then, the days were long and blank. I've learned the art of forgetting.

My mom had hoped she could check me out every Friday so I could come home, but that hope was quashed; there appeared to be no way to manage me, no limit to my resistance. So she decided to transfer me to Kaibeto Boarding School in Kaibeto, Arizona.

Once my mom was resolved to move me, she came midweek to check me out permanently from Tuba City Boarding School. As I waited, desperate to leave this place called school, my mom lifted my small blue suitcase and casually opened it. Abruptly she turned to the dorm staff:

Where are the rest of my daughter's clothes?

The staff member dismissed my mom's question by handing her a document. My mom took it, but then, on a mission, she marched back into the girls' sleeping quarters with me trailing closely behind. She headed straight to the metal wardrobe as the same staff member hurried after us, calling *Wait!* My mom became deaf and shrugged off the woman's pleas, refusing to stop until she had scoured every locker, gathering dresses that I had forgotten about in my misery. She held the dresses and suitcase in one hand and my hand in the other. I ran to keep up with her long strides to the white pickup where my aunt and brother waited.

Yes to getting back my belongings, social justice, but what did these dresses represent to my mom? Maybe she, too, missed the glorious El Monte, with its greenery and mild blues, the convenience of its schools and markets reachable by foot at a strolling pace. Perhaps those lovely dresses that she ransacked lockers to get back were associated with a freedom she also missed.

So, *you've returned to us*, my aunt said with her usual smile.

I never wanted to let my mother and brother out of my sight again. For fear that my mother might change her mind, I quickly became a model of obedience, anticipating her every request. No one had ever called me an angel, but that day I came close. I was allowed to play hooky for the rest of week.

My reprieve wasn't to last. On Sunday, my mom once again washed, ironed, and packed my dresses. I was shined up as before. But this time my mom said I would attend my cousins' Dan and Earl's school, another tribal boarding *olta*. Her reason for transferring me to Kaibeto was *doo nilhats'iid da*. I had become so homesick at the first school that authorities notified her I wasn't well.

Before leaving home again, I asked my dad to repeat certain phrases in English, so I could communicate with the staff. How do I say, *I will be sick? Dishkooh?* How do I say, *I want to see my mom?* In truth I already knew these expressions, but I wanted a guarantee that I would be listened to. I asked my dad, *Will you come to check me out?* His response was no surprise, as he seemed to have relegated all education-related authority to my mom early on: *It depends on your mom.*

My parents' bond had metamorphosed beyond recognition. My mom walked past my dad without acknowledging him. My dad might have been my distant uncle or a stranger. My brother and I now turned to our mom when my dad gave orders. The roles had indeed shifted.

The school that my cousin brothers and sisters attended was in an isolated area. During the drive there, I sat in the back of the pickup with my other windblown cousins, Leonard, Venne, and Dan. The air brushed against us as we huddled under blankets, but having them near made me brave. The mood was jovial, and I felt safe. As we drove east, I expected at every turn or curve that we had reached our destination, but we continued on. I tried to memorize the route. When I eventually gave up, we came to a full stop. We had arrived. I soon learned that two of my cousin brothers lived in the dormitory where I would live.

This time, my mom requested that my clothes be properly labeled with my name. I saw *Evelyn B.* printed on all my clothing except my socks. The dorm mother said they were impossible to match, but she assured my mom that I would have socks. This staff member chatted amiably with my mom. She admired my mom's coat and jewelry. She smiled at me, and being easily impressed, I returned her smiles. She showed my mom where I would sleep and my mom unpacked my clothes. My mom also gave the staff member loose change for my canteen card. This too was recorded. I promptly forgot about this because the idea of putting money into an account was still beyond my six-year-old grasp.

Saying goodbye to my mom was a peaceful exchange. She held me and touched my crown and this time I heard:

Take care of your thoughts and yourself.

I nudged my head against my mom the way a dog or a lamb nuzzles, having evidently forgiven her trespasses. Early signs of my life-long idiotic optimism.

As I hurried to a great window to see my mom walk away, I could still smell her powdery fragrance. Sweet molecules hung in the air as she departed from this new and hopeful setting that held so much promise. I turned to look at the opposite side of the large room, saw my cousin Dan's face, and felt that I could manage myself here.

When more girls returned, I saw a cluster of them singing the alphabet song. Seated on a vinyl bench, they huddled and swung their feet in time to the rhythmic chant. When they finished, they giggled and started the song again. Soon, a tall woman with a big hair bun rang a hand-held bell. On this cue, the girls and boys wordlessly formed a line in their sections. I joined them and we walked to the cafeteria. I followed and mimicked the behavior of the girls nearest to me.

The meal was hot: a meat dish, two sides of vegetables, a roll with a butter square on waxed paper, and a carton of milk. Everyone ate. I picked at what I liked until one girl near me warned, *You have to eat everything.*

I've always been a slow eater. Some of it was due to my endless opinions on everything, but even without a word to anyone here, I couldn't eat. Although a vigilant cafeteria worker monitored the dining room, my cousin Dan suddenly appeared by my side and scooped up what I didn't finish, swiping the butter against his teeth to help clear my plate. Without a single word, he hurried back to his table.

That evening I met my bunk mate. She had short hair and a shrill chastising grandma voice. I heard more the next morning. Over time, I learned to let Effie make her bed first before I tried because to make hers, she had to walk on the metal rack to pull and pinch the corners in of her bed-making. She was a tidy person who barked commands. *Wash your face and brush your teeth while I make my bed. Come over here, I'll braid your hair.* She smoothed out the ripples and lumps in my bed with a few tugs. She helped me dress.

When my mom dressed me, all I had to do was raise my arms in the air for her to slip my clothes on over my head, so dressing myself was an adjustment. No wonder the girls at Tuba City Boarding School took my dresses. I didn't know how to put them on or take them off. Effie, with her no-nonsense grandmother ways, helped. I must have been the younger sister she missed, since she soon adopted me.

Effie was a natural leader. When she couldn't braid my hair, she told another girl to fix it. We lived according to a schedule that Effie had mastered. We got up, made our beds, dressed, groomed, and lined up for breakfast.

Breakfast was another speed-eating contest. We marched directly from there to the classroom. Only knowing that Dan and Earl were somewhere in the building settled my jitters.

I was classified as a *Beginner*, which in other schools would have been called a first grader. I met my teacher, a tall lanky man who introduced himself as Mr. Burt. My clattering nerves kept me from hearing the /t/ sound in his name. Instead, I heard a /d/ sound so called him Mr. Bird. From then I christened him *Tsidii Neez*. Tall Bird. This might be considered name-calling, but I gave him a Navajo name because I liked him. He welcomed me to his room, showed me where I would sit, and like all teachers, assessed my skills.

He separated me from the other students and showed me an abacus. It was framed like my mom's loom and the movement was horizontal, so naturally I liked this new gadget. Methodically he isolated one bead at a time, counting aloud to ten. He waited for me to repeat what he modeled. Then he increased the counting to 20, and I did that, too. Next he separated a bead and said *One*, added two more beads and said *Two*, and asked how many beads were there. I answered *Three*.

Soon he used larger numbers. Satisfied with that, he separated two beads at a time and asked, *How many are there?* He kept me counting by twos until I reached 20, then moved on to threes. He increased to fours, and that's when I stumbled. He finished our short lesson with a single word--*Good*, and sent me back to my seat. Tall Bird's lesson in skipping numbers made me see their magical side, as well as their resemblance to a bouncing ball. Before transitioning to our next exercise, he handed me a sheet of paper with twos, threes, and fours in increasing order, only this time my destination was 20 and 21. These numbers, too, rose with every new sheet.

In reading, we were given copies of the *Dick and Jane* series. If there was phonics, I don't recall. We read over and over until some of us memorized the pages. Mr. Bird emphasized prosody. When we didn't speak with the lilt or lift up our words, he repeated the exercise until we demonstrated subtle improvements. Our class was no different than most. We did our teacher bidding as long as we were met with justice, compassion, and challenge. My nickname *Tsidii Neez* for Mr. Burt was all about appreciation.

For many of us, words we learned in *Tsidii Neez*'s class were new words in our mouths, so we pronounced them as our teacher did. Three such words were *vase, either,* and *neither*. Mr. Bird pronounced vase with an /uh/ sound and he used a long /i/ in either and neither. There were other words that I didn't try to make sense of. If *Tsidii Neez* wanted us to say it a particular way, we did.

My first morning was soon over, and we formed a line to go to lunch. I tried to finish what was on my plate, and when I couldn't, the Dans of the table helped me. There was some bartering and some promises were made, but I agreed and, my clean plate passed inspections.

Instead of returning to the classroom, we marched back to the dormitory sleeping quarters, and I watched the others remove their dresses and hang them in their wardrobes. I fought with my dress and somehow won without tearing any seams. Then I saw the girls go to their beds, lie down and close their eyes. It was miraculous that they could fall asleep so fast. As I watched others, Effie whispered *niishch'iil*. I shut my eyes and welcomed sleep. The tinging of the hand-held bell woke us. As they dressed, Effie and another girl helped yank my dress down. We marched in a line back to the classrooms.

Rest period didn't always go this smoothly. The tall woman with the big hair bun yelled at us for what seemed like tiny infractions. How any of us slept in those conditions was a mystery, but a few did. I did. I closed my eyes and transported myself home to my family and familial comforts, and I was out.

More than once before the bell sounded, I awoke to see a line of girls bending over as Big Hair Bun Woman swung her lanyard and snapped struck their bottoms. Some girls burst into tears before the dreaded sting, but others managed sharp intakes of air and bore the abuse in silence. I looked at the girls who cried before the lanyard struck. I decided they wouldn't make great friends because they might crumble away easily. Then I studied the faces of the stoics, admiring them for their heroism. I had never before considered the complexity of how we bow to an oppressor. The girls who blubbered prematurely got a milder whipping than the steel-faced girls. Then again, the stoic girls had had years of abuse, and the whipping was merely an inconvenience. It never occurred to me that these more hardened girls might mete out their anger on me merely for having the misfortune of standing in front of them in line. I knew so little.

It was Friday, and on Fridays the children who didn't get checked out to go home watched a movie. And just maybe, just maybe we might have popcorn. I associated popcorn with carnivals or parties, and I tingled with excitement. During nap period, I couldn't sleep. I just lay on my bunk bed staring at the wall, a partition dividing each bunkbed, confident that Big Hair Bun wouldn't catch me. I could hear her patrolling for fake-sleepers. Every once in a while, I heard a girl's name being called, then the sound of rustling and bare feet padding on the linoleum. Some girls sighed loudly. I clenched my eyes shut when I heard the clacking steps of Big Hair Bun She paused nearby, studying a face or listening to breathing. I hadn't realized how many others faked sleep by staring at the partition between the bunkbeds. I heard Big Hair Bun approaching me, and in that instant, I noticed my lips were dry, probably a nervous response. Then an itch formed in the corners of my mouth. Popcorn. Maybe we'd be given brown paper bags of popcorn instead of an adult handful on a sheet of butcher paper that we ate in budgeted mouthfuls. Well, some did. I ate mine in two or three handfuls. I pressed my lips together tightly, forgetting how close Big Hair Bun was.

Get up, she ordered.

I sighed. It had been just a matter of time. I took my place in line and bent over like the others. Big Hair Bun moved on.

When she was out of sight, some brave girls stood up and stretched. I didn't. Once I was in line, I let my popcorn fantasy play out full blast.

It wasn't long before I heard the peal of her bell. Big Hair Bun always waited for the rest of the sleepers to wake up before she returned to whip the bad actors or those with a streak of recklessness. Her very effective strategy was a warning to all of the consequences of not sleeping during nap time. One by one, she struck each behind. If a girl flinched too soon, she got the thighs, or worse, a stinging punishment to the back. As Big Hair Bun approached from the right, I glanced reflexively in her direction; close up, what I had thought was smooth skin was pock marked. She wore red lip color. Her hair was long, long enough for the buffalo-patty sized bun. Her wrist was creased by the narrow strip of her gold-toned watch. Her lanyard was a leather braid. One minute she held the keys in order to whip girls with the leather, the next she wore the whip around her neck.

When she neared me, I clinched my eyes shut and steeled myself. I heard the lanyard cut the air and felt the leather meet my bottom. Through my panties my butt stung, but now anger burned as well. The sight of the whip encircling her neck like a victory medal outraged my six-year-old sense of dignity.

Afterwards, I put on my dress without Effie's or anyone else's help. Any interest in movie night and popcorn had evaporated. I longed to tell my mom. I pictured her fury. I had gotten my share of butt snaps or an occasional pinch, but only by my parents. No one else had ever hit me.

My first shower at my new boarding school was yet another initiation. The little girls, like me, shared a stall with two others. We had two bars of soap and shampoo was dispensed in small dabs. If the spray of water washed it from our hands, we used the Castile soap bar to wash our hair. It was a noisy affair with cries that transformed into giggles. Some girls were afraid of the spray of water because it ran cold and then suddenly hot. At home, I normally loved showers, or in our case, sponge baths or when we all took turns bathing in a portable steel tub. It was a wonderful part of the evening, the signal for sleep and the blissful nightly slumber among my family members.

Pick up the soap, a staff person commanded. *Wash your ears.*

Heavy steps sounded through the showering noises. Then a male voice—*Hello girls.*

I turned to my showering mates to see their reactions. One girl's eyes were closed as she washed her hair, but the other leaned out to giggle, as did a few more nearby. I stepped in the far corner to hide. A man was in the shower room. No one seemed alarmed. Some returned his greeting.

He started from one end of the stalls calling out the names of various girls. I heard his boots on the cement floor and his jiggling keys. Always the keys. Instead of the chastising voices, his was soft. The sound of his footsteps grew louder as he came closer.

Hold still. That's right. Beautiful.

He was taking pictures. The rapid-fire shutter clicks paused briefly, then repeated again and again. I heard an *Oh my* or two before he reached our stall.

Hello, sweetheart.

His voice was syrupy sweet. And he smiled too much.

I hid behind the two girls, but they parted, so I could see him. His red wavy hair. The freckles and the lines on his face. He lifted his camera to his eye and took several pictures of my companions and me. They giggled, but I was mute. A man was in the shower room. The staff member was just here a moment ago. Surely she saw him walk in this direction. Where was she? Did she leave to report him?

That must be it.

The man's camera clicked a few more times and then he moved on.

I was wrong. No one reported the man with the camera. He came again and again.

Sometimes he came while Big Hair Bun was supervising. Sometimes they bent their heads together, chuckling. She never objected to his presence. In our most intimate moments of dormitory life, we were violated. Sleep and showering. She never shielded us. In fact, to ease his way, she separated us from the older girls' stalls farther away. That was where he spent much of his time.

The year before, my parents had taken Dean and me to get photographed in El Monte. As they looked on, the photographer positioned me behind my brother. I held him. Alway charming, Dean smiled. As long as I sheltered behind my brother, I felt secure, but even that didn't translate into a smile for me. The photographer cajoled me with *Smile! Smile dear*, and waved a stuffed animal in our faces. Still no smile. He took a few pictures of Dean by himself, and my brother posed obediently. But when it was my turn, the photographer began to prod me with the stuffed animal. First, he aimed at my face, so I fidgeted out of his way. Then he took the animal and tapped various parts of my torso as he made moronic adult noises. When he started to bat the crumpled toy at my chest, I blocked him. I raised my right arm like a vertical beam to protect my chest and used my left arm to hold my other in place. I struck a thinking pose. Flash. He captured that image of my protest. At five, my nipples were sensitive to this outrage; flat and insignificant as my chest was, I could feel the brush of the toy bring my nipples to life. It didn't feel right, and the invasion by this man and his stuffed animal felt even more wrong.

I had no pleasant connections with picture-taking by strangers. My mom, the family documentarian, brought her camera wherever we went, and I never objected to that. Exception of her requests, I struck stiff or silly poses; I tolerated her photos.

However, this new man with his camera in the shower stalls was a malign, vile presence. I sensed that he focused more on the pretty girls or whichever of their attributes appealed to him. Sometimes he posed the girls, most often the compliant smiling ones. To avoid his attention, as soon as I heard his boots, I lathered and rubbed soap suds into my eyes. This produced a rage of tears, but though he paused at our stall, he usually moved on unless he noticed another girl. I never giggled or smiled. Sometimes I turned from acknowledging him, but even then he might take a quick picture for good measure before advancing to the next stall.

At six, I already knew about the poverty of power. If I couldn't depend on adults at the boarding school to fulfill their obligations, I could at least shield myself from what I knew to be wrong—more than wrong—a violation and a sickening crime.

The image of a different kind of adult I studied was a white-robed, bearded Jesus sitting on a rock with a child on his lap and more children surrounding him. He appeared to lean in, listening intently to the child on his lap. Examining this picture, I wondered what the little person had said that held Jesus's attention. It must have been engrossing because Jesus could have been out walking on water, calming the storms, raising the dead, or vandalizing the temples, but instead chose to be here—with children thronging to him, rapt and attentive. He didn't have the patronizing look I sometimes saw on adults' faces when they listened to a child. My image of Jesus—an earnest, kind-looking man—was on a page of a book that was miles away in my parents' home, but I relied on the image whenever I surged with anger, hatred, and deadly wishes. I couldn't make sense of my feelings, but concentrating on that image, however idealized, calmed the seething emotions that filled my chest and made my eyes hurt and ears drum.

Who could I tell about this terrifying routine enacted almost daily in our dormitory? At the time, I was too young to even imagine what the photographer might have been doing to the older girls in their dorm. I couldn't envision what he did to those he bribed with candy bars or other pitiful enticements, all the furtive losses of innocence and the anger, shame, and despair they'd engendered. It would take even longer for me to realize how many of those girls were caught up in the circulation of that abuse as adults. For a six-year-old, the consequences for the nameless multitude of Navajo girls were beyond comprehension.

I called the shower photographer Mr. Carrot. I couldn't pronounce his name, and my only protest was to ignore him. When we were in the main dormitory, when he was cameraless, I managed to disregard his sickeningly sweet, cajoling voice. I couldn't understand how he was regarded with something like deference by children and staff. He was more frightening than the *Stranger Danger* offenders we were taught about in kindergarten because this man worked on site, and on any given day he could abuse his role and invade girls' privacy or entice children into his office. I despised his *I want to be friends* bait that lured these children into the zone behind his closed door.

Out of the blue, I contracted chicken pox, and as far as I know I was the only patient. I was quarantined in a small room with a single bed, accustomed to attending classes, eating in the dining hall, and sleeping in the dormitory, I found solitude hard to take. Bereft of society, hearing outside life taunted and tormented me. I cried a lot. I also feared that

Mr. Carrot might use this opportunity to try to befriend me. Luckily for me, he had plenty of healthy girls to choose from.

I had fought for life and become angry about life, but being isolated introduced me to a new despair. I wanted to die, not from the discomfort of chicken pox, but from my confinement in that room. In my own Navajo language, when I constructed sentences involving play, learning, walking, or even sleeping, I used the first person plural. Thinking or using t'*aasahi*, a *by myself* reference, was an unfamiliar, foreign concept. The idea of the collective whole was imprinted in my thoughts, speech, and action. Years later when I read *Jane Eyre*, I felt her punishment in the red room as my own. At the time, if I were told that the transition from life to death would be as easy as closing my eyes, I would have welcomed it. I entertained myself by playing dead when food was brought in or when a nurse checked my temperature or gauged my health. I decided death was the only option if I had to stay in this room by myself any longer.

I eventually recovered. However revolted I had been by the picture-taking of Mr. Carrot and his picture taking and Big Hair Bun's butt-whipping for not sleeping on demand, after my internment, I welcomed my return to society. I would not relent in any way—Mr. Carrot and Big Hair Bun would continue to be the enemy—but I wanted to be back among my peers.

In late spring, we took our first school field trip. We filed onto a school bus after being divided into two groups: blue birds and yellow birds. I was a yellow bird. Our destination was Flagstaff, Arizona—properly named, *Kinlani* meaning *many buildings*.

As usual, I welcomed whatever this trip would yield. I enjoyed the mystery of getting on a bus in one setting and getting off in another. The Navajo word for travel is *ch'aana'ada*. It connotes walking, probably because we walked from one place to another in the days before horse or wagon ownership. So, to be able to get into a vehicle, in this case a bus, and be transported from Kaibeto to Flagstaff, involved considerable invention. I had only traveled great distances in the care of my parents, so this indeed was an adventure. We stopped for lunch at another boarding school in Flagstaff. Then, as we settled back in our seats on the bus, I happened to glance at the dormitory we had just visited. In the second floor window, I spotted an older boy and girl looking out at us. They smiled, so I waved a cheerful hello to them. They smiled back, and then as the boy waved, he raised his middle finger at me. His friend caught the gesture and laughed. I didn't know what the finger meant, but her laughter suggested that neither was as friendly as I had hoped. Someone else on the bus must have observed the boy, and when I heard an *Oh my*, I knew I was right.

Later that day, I was the butt of yet another mean gesture. This time the offender was an adult. When we reached the train station, we visited the restroom. I was one of the first to use the toilet. At the time, public toilet use cost a dime in high traffic areas, so the easy bypass involved having the short girls do what I did, crawl under the door. I hadn't heard the instructions, probably something like, *Crawl in and do your business*, *but unlock the stall door for the next person.* Simple, but I didn't hear that. I just heard, *Crawl under, Evelyn.*

I remember the grime and buildup in the grout between the tiles and the dust and lint sticking to the base of the white toilet. I didn't consider the filth on my hands, knees, and clothing, doing only as I was told in the echo-y sounding lavatory.

When I got on all fours to creep back out under the stall door, I heard my name in the echo chamber, and then I got kicked on the head with a big shoe. That evidently was the most efficient way to get my attention. Yet I didn't hear any derisive laughter, so I reversed course and stood up and opened the stall door for the next girl to use the facility. If I felt wounded, I don't recall; to me, this was just another instance of instruction by Kaibeto Boarding School staff. Just another day in boarding school.

Later, seated beside another girl on our long awaited train ride, I marveled at how quickly the landscape changed, from mountainous pines to reddish hills formed by ancient volcanic activity, to scattered cedars before the land smoothed to a prairie of yellow straw under the expansive blue sky. The ride was even and comfortable and only the periodic track shift sound reminded me we were on a train. The Navajo word for train combines fire and wagon, *ko' na'albaasii*, so the word has power. Imagine how this made some of us feel. We were moving with the spirit of fire. Besides having Tall Bird as my first-grade teacher, this was the third highlight in a tumultuous year.

The second was getting a rag doll in a calico dress and apron with brown skin and black hair tied in a proper bun. Tall Bird explained that his fiancée—another new word in our mouths—sewed the dolls, which every girl received. When I received mine, I was enchanted, feeling that she had been waiting for me. That young woman fiancée must have loved Tall Bird, and perhaps us, too. My world increased in size now that someone in Pennsylvania knew and cared about me. Having a mom who sewed and wove, I studied the seams, and I could see that this was sewn with a sewing machine because the stitches were even. I admired everything about the doll, how she molded in my arms and how she stared wide-eyed at the world. Later when we moved into our newly built Navajo tribal three-roomed house, I pinned her to my wall next to the top of the bunkbed where I slept. She looked at me day and night for years. Every time we came home from Phoenix for a weekend getaway, she was there waiting patiently for me.

At this boarding school, while I had the comforts of my cousin brothers nearby, the only time I saw and talked with them was during recess. This remained my favorite time of the day. I was already awakened earlier than the other girls because I was a slow eater. By then my hair was shorn to a bob because I couldn't take care of it. I didn't know how to wash or braid it well. The cogs of the boarding school schedule didn't permit a break in the pace of the system. A bob was the wash and wear style for a slow eater.

Up until that time, I hadn't resorted to any physical protests in response to small daily injuries. Out of earshot, I heard occasional verbal beatings. *Stupid, dim-wit, shut up, your anus,* or, the absolute worst, *Go back to hell.* Sometimes someone penciled the word kiss on the interior of someone's metal wardrobe locker. When Big Hair Bun made this discovery on the locker door of gentle little-scared-faced Lilly, she had us stand around as she opened the door to point to the offending word. I marveled how a four-letter word could draw this much attention. I knew the meaning of kiss, but I wondered if it had a deeper meaning I didn't know. Kiss was raised to even greater, filthier heights, according to the dorm staff, when it ended with a Y. Kissy. *Oh my.* However, as much as I tried to make sense of punishments, I still saw them as arbitrary. One day a person made a big to-do about an infraction, but the next day, it was no longer an infraction. The following week, it was once again a boarding school sin.

Poor Lilly. She was an easy target because she cried easily; her eyes always looked ready to betray her. She was a gentle person who gave up her swing or made room for me on the monkey bars. I don't recall how fast she ran, but I'd guess she was a speedy athlete. She would have had to be because she was picked on by so many. Not by me but many others; still, I might have been part of the taunting mass, in Lilly's eyes.

When boarding school anger and missing-home blues rose to a whistling kettle heat, we lashed out at each other. A quick hair yanking of an unsuspecting victim walking by; a swift kick that earned an offender bonus points if the kick resulted in a fall; or a smarting pinch. I knew of pinching, thanks to my mom. I took some abuse, but I didn't get much as far as I remember. I'm sure Effie had a role in this. Dear Effie. When I stood in line after recess, I got a quick grooming under her deft fingers, along with her chastisement. Her voice was harsh but her touch was gentle.

She couldn't protect me when few of us slowpoke eaters marched early to the cafeteria for breakfast. One taller girl had a really nice smile. Whenever we caught one another's eyes, she always smiled, forever gullible, I always returned my best ambassador smile. She situated herself right across from me and just as I started eating, she gave me swift kick to my right shin. There was no way to avoid her good-morning kick. She stood behind whomever sat across from me until the girl rose and found a new seat, vacating the spot for Kicking Girl. I'm sure she bullied others, but she dedicated herself to me every morning. Before, during and after her kick, she invariably smiled. Smiling Kicking Girl was bigger than I was, and I was quiet. Easy picking. I began to dread breakfast. Sometimes I waited for her kick before starting to eat, surrendering.

My mom's admonishment to take care of my thoughts meant acting with kindness, dignity, and obedience, but her words receded with Smiling Kicking Girl's every kick. When my cousin brothers saw my bruised shins, they instructed me to kick back and to hit her hard, too. *Wait until no one is looking or when you're alone with her*, they counseled.

By then I had learned that adults didn't rescue or protect children. When Lilly was picked on and cried, she was called

Crybaby by adults and girls alike, punished for her own victimization. In my case, Effie was the only one in my corner. She was one of the tall girls.

I didn't plan my protest, but one morning, Smiling Kicking Girl camped out in front of me grinning as usual, but before she swung her foot to make contact with me, I kicked her unsuspecting shin. She had offered me the perfect bull's-eye and her own repeated modeling. Once I kicked her, I could feel that visceral pleasure of brute triumph. Then I kicked her again. This was pure evil on my part. After each kick, I smiled at her. The next morning, I gave her two more fast reminders. When she found her new seat the following morning, I poked out my face to display a smile. Later when I followed her into the sleeping quarters, I pulled her braids and swung her head into the cinderblock wall like I was reining in a horse to a sudden stop.

Maybe those Bible stories that my dad read to us fed my keen guilt and personal shame. I knew I hadn't represented my mother well. The constant ache for her weighed on me less because I was in Tall Bird's class. He brought order to numbers, letters, and words for much of my day, but I had to contend with Mr. Carrot, Big Hair Bun, and other indifferent staff for the remainder of every 24 hours—creating a weird, tottering imbalance. When I fought back, I was aware that a long line of adults still threatened me. I couldn't kick or pull their hair. My future assailants had featureless faces and loomed large in my imagination.

Around this time, I developed a recurring dream, one with a nightmarish quality. I loved adding and subtracting two digits. I knew I was good at it because I was one of the first to finish and get to play on the abacus in class. My dream began with single digit numbers landing together for me to add. This was the fun, easy step, but the more I added, the faster the numbers would fall, dropping from an unknown space high above me. The ceiling or sky was cloudy and shadowy. The numbers were three dimensional, and I sat at a wooden desk as I added them. Sometimes I had a sheet of paper and a pencil to write the answers. The nightmare involved the single digits becoming two and three digits, and I had to add three sets of numbers. Eventually I couldn't keep up, so the numbers stacked up like Tetris. The problems grew and grew like the Tower of Babel. Sometimes the numbers tumbled on me, and sometimes I woke up just as they began to sway high above me before their inevitable collapse.

One day during recess, I made my way from the other children to an older, unused part of the playground. My shame and guilt made even my favorite playground distractions, the swings, merry-go-round, and monkey bars, insignificant. I sat on a curb and sang a made-up song, but I when I sang what became the chorus, I stood up and faced the direction where I imagined my mom to be. My words had power. I could see them vibrating in waves on the vortex of the winds and light. I sang my song in Navajo, knowing that my words would reach her:

My mother, my mother, my mother
I'm thinking of you, my mother.

Remember me, remember me.
Return to me please. Please.

Before I knew it, my tears spilled down my face, my shoulders shook, and my heavy heart quaked. When I felt the release of all that bottled up pressure, my tears subsided, and I sighed a great clean exhalation. My swollen eyelids felt better closed, but my breath flowed so freely, so exuberantly from my chest that I broke into the chorus of Credence Clearwater Revival's "Proud Mary." I didn't understand all the lyrics, but one line rang out clearly, proclaiming the kindness of strangers. If someone sang this, then surely some generous people really did exist out there in the adult world. Somewhere.

I believed once I was in my mom's arms, I would recover from whatever had stained me. Her love would cleanse me.

Finally, school came to an end. From the moment other girls began whispering about that day, I thought about nothing else. Even Big Hair Bun with her singing, stinging lanyard had no power to ruin the prospect of our approaching freedom. However, as luck would have it, no one came for my cousin brothers or me. No uncle from my many kinship relations. No one.

On the big day, my cousin brother Dan, a few others who lived near us, and I were packed into a van to be shipped home. What a day. The canteen change that my mother had long ago deposited for me to spend on sweets was returned to me in a small envelope. I was told to keep it sealed, but that fell on deaf ears, and I opened it. I knew quarters and pennies, but nickels and dimes baffled me. How could a big thick nickel be worth less than a small skinny dime? Needless to say, I traded all my dimes for nickels with a tall girl. My cousin brother Dan looked on as I robbed myself, but the joy and merriment of going home was all that mattered to us.

When we were still far from our destination, I began searching for my family's small black house. By today's standard, our home could easily be a tool or storage shed. But I had no idea it was small. It held all of us, so to me it was plenty large.

When we came closer, I didn't recognize our house, which had stood alone in the past. Now, nearby was an unfamiliar white structure with a red roof. I was puzzled, wondering whether Dan and I had somehow been transported to another time. The surrounding sand bank, sandstones, and ridges were definitely our home place, but where did that house come from?

The van slowed to a stop and my mom came out of the white house to meet us. When I burst from the van, she folded me into her arms. I smelled her. She appeared to be her. My brother joined us. What a reunion.

Where did this come from? I marveled how the edges of the white house had two cedar bushes.

My mom took me inside. The walls were lavender and the floor was a checkerboard of speckled royal blue and white linoleum. In her boots, my mom's steps sounded confident. The house had a table and chairs and what I perceived as immense counters with shelves. She showed me where the stove and refrigerator would soon be and where Dean and I would sleep. My parents' old bed from the black house had been moved to the new house. The house had six windows to let in plenty of light. It had two doors, but instead of facing the holy east direction, one faced south and the other west. I could smell the pines. I walked on my heels with my toes lifted just to hear my steps. It was a satisfying sound.

While I attended Kaibeto Boarding School, my mom had continued to weave, but she had added a new activity to her daily routine. Every morning, she readied my bother Dean to attend kindergarten at a day school in Coppermine. He took a spare set of clothes for his just-in-case moments as he climbed onto the bus, driven by John. This particular John was an honored figure in my mother's eyes because he picked up and delivered my brother Dean back to her every day. My mom undoubtedly measured Dean's happy daily reunion with her as a sign of academic progress. It was different from my own kindergarten experience in El Monte, but my mom had accustomed herself to the tribal educational system, although, as it turned out, it would not be for long.

Before the new house had been built for our family, my parents had attended many evening meetings at the chapter house. Mom was a confident weaver and having lived in California gave her additional self-assurance. She may not have had her once happy marriage, but she could speak clearly on our family's behalf to petition to have built, by my standards, this huge house that we started to call the White House. *Kinligai*. Equally wonderful was that my Aunt Jessie Ma and Uncle Guy Billy had a house even bigger than ours. Teen Bi

Masani had one, too. While I was away, our small nestled homestead had transformed small homes into larger ones. My great-grandmother Lola had a one room hogan-styled house built for her, too. But she still had her cupboard with the green curtain and no furniture.

The amount allocated by the Navajo tribe to each family depended on the number of household members, but the figure also included furnishings. My mom decided on a smaller house so that she could purchase furniture. All in one day, she chose a bunk bed, a queen-sized mattress with a frame, a dresser, a chest of drawers and a table and chairs. My Uncle Kee Nez Begay delivered the load from Flagstaff. I felt like we lived in a mansion. However, as much as the exterior of our lives changed, my parents weren't in a happier place. My dad still wandered off for days. Finding him home in the evening and waking to find him still at home were good days. My mom still wove, and we still collected monthly government commodities, the Navajo version of public assistance.

If my dad wasn't home for lunch or dinner, my mom sometimes made my favorite food, peanut butter mixed with jelly smeared on her handmade naan-like tortilla, which she folded and cut in half. If he was home, she made fried potatoes with commodity meat, stringy strands of cooked flesh that came sealed in a steel can. Sometimes my mom bought bacon and a carton of eggs that she stored in a covered box and kept in the cool cabinet. On the mornings my dad was home, my mom fried him bacon and eggs with potatoes. For special days, she opened a can of peaches for my brother and me to sup with a tortilla. These meals were delicious. I am still an easy-to-please eater. I still love peanut butter, which is a food group for me. Peanut butter or nut butters on celery, apples, baby spinach, or in my green salad. Still as delicious as when I first tasted it.

My mom also made wonderful bread with a can of creamed corn. She poured the can right into the bread mix before kneading it. Then she stretched the dough into a sheet as she tossed it from palm to palm, stretching and growing with each transfer. She didn't toss it in the air as shown in TV-land pizzerias, but she made a thin bread dough that she placed into a hot cast iron pan or right on the open-fire grill. That's my favorite bread. We ate the bread by itself. Too good for any topping.

When I was much older and visiting my mom, I asked her to make that same creamed corn bread. She chafed at my request to make bread that was bare-cupboard-time eating. I had no idea. I prodded her, telling her that her bread was special, and that even by fancy bakery standards her bread was nowhere else to be found. If I saw a cafe with that sort of bread on its menu, I'd buy it in a heartbeat. *Ah, I know you, friend. Come to me.* The ingenuity of mothers finding a way feed their children. These inventions gave birth to stories and yearnings for a rich past when life was reimagined as simpler.

During a visit to Gap Trading Post that summer, we poured out of my Aunt Sadie's pickup and observed a big van with RIF written on it in the parking lot. I ventured near and stood at the door smiling, expecting to be invited in. It worked. A young woman and man welcomed me inside, followed by my cousins, Venne, Dan, Marilyn, and my brother Dean. RIF was the abbreviation for Reading Is Fun, and this was the book-mobile. We were allowed to get one book each, although, somehow, I got two. While my cousins might have chosen theirs simply to please the couple, I chose painstakingly. Kneeling at the lower shelves, I wanted a book I could read several times, not just to myself but to my brother and mother and anyone else who wanted to listen. Illustrations were nice, but I wanted a story that would last, one that was reusable many times over. I had learned to read well enough to know its magic, its ability to transport me to far-away places. This brief visit to the book-mobile signaled that my life might be forking from my relatives, but like many significant moments, this was hardly noticeable, like minute sun positions in a summer sky. While I clasped mine and my brother's books in my arms when it was time to return from the trading post, I saw one of the newly chosen books with its jacket cover fluttering in the wind on the truck bed. Abandoned, forgotten.

Relatives might have thought my mom spoiled us, but it's the way someone who comes from a large family remembers hunger, the lack of privacy, the crowding into a small space. My mother recalled the attention she had craved, and how her parents were always gazing far away, somewhere other than where their responsibility lay. She wanted children she could watch and raise. Of course, I was still in primary school—adorable, trusting, with a worshipful quality she appreciated. I wouldn't always have this, so she let us run and play when others my age already worked. She sewed our blankets, curtains, and her clothes and, if she could, she bought me a dress or two. I don't ever recall her sitting still unless she was weaving, but if anyone has ever seen a weaver at work, there's nothing stationary about this skilled artist.

Somewhere around this time, I learned my mom's first name. I knew my dad's first name, Fred, but gradually I began to hear *Elsie* this and *Elsie* that in accusatory, caustic tones. I sensed that the alchemy of family dynamics was changing; it was too subtle to name, but I felt the difference.

In the evenings, after dinner, sometimes my mom, brother, and I walked to my Aunt Sadie's. It was lovely summer, and we walked home under a moon that lighted our way and seemed magically big. I believed that everything was for me—sunny days, moonlit or moonless nights—everything.

In the morning, when I washed my hands and slapped water on myself, I was so sloppy that my mom resorted to washing me. She once again treated me with princess status. She took a wash cloth, lathered the bar of soap, placed the bar on a dish, and then wiped my neck, my hair line, arms and face and hands. She covered her index finger with the cloth and swabbed my ears. All I had to do was stand still and wait until the polishing was over. Newly washed, I felt the sun's rays touch every pore and fill me with light. The cool morning air followed with its second cleansing, bathing me in its very own nature. I heard birds sing and fly from cedar trees to bushes. Mornings were glorious at home. My mom's attention was restored to me. By then I had pinned the rag doll given to us by Tall Bird's fiancee to my wall. These were beautiful days.

One evening I happened to be playing with my cousins, the ones closest to my age, Venne, Dan, and Marilyn. I rarely interacted with the older Leonard, Melvin, and the very oldest, Newland. In fact, I generally stayed away from them. My *Nali* referred to them as *hastoi*. Men. They weren't, but I was ever conscious of how youth changed suddenly from *alchini* to *saanii or hastoi*. I associated the adult roles with height, but beyond that, I was unsure. Somehow I wound up alone with the *hastoi*, my older male cousins in my paternal grandmother's hogan. Maybe it started out as a game, but it quickly changed. I saw a face looming close and could feel my dress being lifted, then the air on my stomach and thighs when I was on my back, the gritty, harden earth that we walked on as family members. The bare hogan earth scraped my back and butt. The movements were fierce. How long was it? I don't think it was long enough for me to scream, but I must have. When it was over, I stumbled out in a fog of burning and tearing pain. I didn't know what had happened. I still don't. I have no recollection of details. I crept to my mom, who was in the middle of a conversation with my Aunt Sadie and *Nali*. I moaned, *It hurts, Mom*, but she brushed me off her lap. The sun must have set hours before, so she couldn't see my bare legs or stained dress. I sat near her and looked towards the hogan where I had been injured, to the rising moon, and all around me at what until then had seemed another perfect summer night.

We walked home later. The pain throbbed unbearably with each step, but holding my mom's hand was soothing as we trudged the half mile. I felt like boarding school had followed me home.

Only when she bathed me that night did she see the bloody effects of my torn hymen. Normally she used a kerosene lamp to light the area in the kitchen where she sponge-bathed my brother and me. Heating the water on the wood burning stove made the house glow with warmth, like it breathed and cooed us. Very cozy. But even the glow couldn't alter what I had experienced. That soft light wasn't enough. Needing better lighting, she used her flashlight. She murmured *shiyazhi, shiyazhi, ashineh* as her eyes filled. She cursed with words I didn't know. Her emotions were always tightly contained, but hearing her I moaned freely, *It hurts so much, Shima*. She asked me for details, but I didn't have the knowledge to explain. I didn't know what had happened to me. I had no language for it. The closest image I could compare to my experience was the writhing of a sheep as it bleats in alarm, right before it is decapitated.

My mom must have settled us to sleep, and then she walked back to my Aunt Sadie's and *Nali*'s to explain what had happened. And it was then that my mom decided to leave that wonderful house with lavender walls and checkered floor, with brand new beds, table, and the bureau with a huge mirror. We still didn't have our gasoline range yet. But she was insistent. She gave my dad an ultimatum, and he took whatever tools he had and a small knapsack to Gap, where he caught a Greyhound to Phoenix. She didn't tell him what had happened to me, not for another 20 years, but her anger was enough for him to act again, as he had years before, when they moved to Oakland.

When my mom explained to the matriarchs what had taken place, my loving and humorous aunt and *Nali* remained silent. The silence was only broken when my mom rose and left. Years before, she had escaped from family violence, fleeing to the only brother she associated with safety. She had protected herself then. But a wind drafted into our newly-built haven and only steps away from her. She was unable to protect me from injury unimaginable to her, or maybe she knew about these violations. My mom held much.

This incident changed everything for us. We no longer visited my aunt or other relatives. My mom kept us home. She burned my stained lime green dress with the gathered waist band, as well as my underwear.

Later my father sent money for our bus fares. We packed very little—our iron pan, a few clothes, along with bread that my mom folded into a dish linen for the bus. So few material objects but enough to start over again in a new setting.

When the bus pulled into the Phoenix bus terminal, I smelled stale cigarette smoke and diesel exhaust. It was the smell of people cooped up in a small container, exuding all the scents of expectation and fear of what lay ahead. We stepped off the bus, and my mom carried our suitcase as we walked out to the noisy, sunny downtown streets of 1971 Phoenix. My mom walked resolutely, while I wondered which way we were headed. Suddenly we found our father walking directly towards us on the same sidewalk. He looked delighted to see us. I was amazed that my mom had known how and where to find my dad; she established her command of the situation as though she were a charging queen on a chess board. Perhaps my dad appreciated my mom's decisiveness. Perhaps he appreciated having her back in his corner.

This magical reunion has a special place in my heart. This was the first time we ate in a restaurant, maybe just a hole-in-the-wall, but a restaurant. The smoky diner's speckled table tops had aluminum edging, and when I ran my hand underneath our table, I felt wads of chewing gum that customer had lodged there just before they ate. The stuck-under-the-table chewing gum and friendly waitress memorialized that meal and promised a new start. I felt that confidently, even in my belly.

The abuses of tribal boarding school and rape were behind me. My dad had returned to us, and we were experiencing the long-awaited burger with fries and a Coke. I invariably gravitate to this meal when I'm not sure what to order. It is still my definition of a true American dream meal.

When I'd swallowed the last of the Busy Bee Cafe burger, I slipped my finger beneath the table, peeled off a wad of gum and popped it in my mouth. My parents seemed to have fallen back in love, so my brother was the only one who noticed I was chewing gum. I divided it to share with him, just to be fair.

CHAPTER 3
Second Grade: Moby Dick

We stayed in a new one-bedroom furnished apartment. My brother and I took turns sleeping on either the couch or floor. Having bought us the elusive burger and fries with a Coke, our parents took us to the grocery store, where we enjoyed our first taste of democracy when our dad invited us to choose our cold cereal, hopeful sign of our former dad returning from afar. We liked being under his dome again. My brother and I negotiated in the cereal aisle amid what seemed like miles of boxes. Our mom, even with no education or nutritional background, said we couldn't choose a sugar-based cereal. She referred to sugar as *dixos*. No glittery sugars. That helped narrow our choices. We finally agreed on Cheerios. We liked the mini donut shapes, and we remembered a commercial we had seen on our small black and white television featuring snow skiers grinning from ear to ear as they flew down sparkling white slopes. We were hopeful that the cereal would inspire the same joy in us. We needed laughter right now. Later when we ate the Cheerios, we giggled, perplexing our parents as they passed timid smiles to one another.

The brief interlude in our compact living space was a mini-party. Dean and I were glued to the TV. My mom, still reeling from my assault, kept me indoors. I couldn't recall any details about the rape when she asked me. I wanted to comply but drew a blank. The trauma might have prevented me from putting a name and face to my violator, my cousin brother, but I did become alert to the lingering gazes of strangers. While blond bike man was easy to categorize as stranger danger, putting my cousin brother in this same category was a mental and social challenge. He possessed the same chromosomes as I did. His mother was my dad's older sister. He was someone from our neck of woods, whom I had thought of as safe and dependable. How this warped my foundation, my sense of family and even of my own my judgment and safety. That was where the true violation lay.

In my imagination, what might have been casual glances were magnified into sinister fixations. It had begun with a man in a car promising me a bike, but now I steered away from all men, unfamiliar or not. While I could not recall the details, my body did, reacting to situations before I was aware of them. I would feel the small hairs on my limbs rise, and I became conscious of my shallow breathing. Somewhere deep, my body registered my experience in detail. Mr. Carrot hadn't helped matters either. That perplexing summer, giggling about cereal; and the world of TV was an easy response.

Even had I not been assaulted, I doubt that my mom would have let us go outside. The Phoenix heat was extreme for Arizona northerners accustomed to heavy snow and four seasons. We all adjusted soon enough, but the first week of stifling heat kept my mom, my brother, and me indoors. Only my father left every morning for his welding job, carrying his metal lunchbox containing two sandwiches and an apple. He was back into the rhythm of work; I know scarcely anyone who loved the routine of work more than my dad, except maybe my mom and my maternal grandmother.

My mom snapped a photo of a visit we took to a nearby park. In the photo I wore a sleeveless, small checkered button-down, and I'm making a scrunched-up-face smile. My bobbed hair is growing out. My head is tilted, my eyes squinted almost shut, and I grinned from ear to ear. I still remember how this felt on my face, and I sometimes strike this pose when I'm playful for the camera. In that long ago picture, was I putting on a happy face for my mom? She was clearly jarred by my violation and, while I luxuriantly buried my experience, she was still reeling from it. Maybe she harbored guilt that she had been unable to protect me, maybe it reminded her of a packed-away violation of her younger self, or maybe her husband's family's inaction amplified my father's absence and she blamed him for it. He had failed us and would do so, again and again. I have another possible explanation for this exaggerated shut-eye-wild-grin pose: I was teaching myself to be happy again. Perhaps I too felt guilt for having caused such a stir, enough to make my dad pack up his tools, walk to Gap, catch a bus, and have us follow in his footsteps to Phoenix. The assault changed the trajectory of our family.

The small apartment, initially ideal for our lone dad, was too small for all of us, and no school was nearby. Party-time for Dean and me ended after a couple of weeks, when we made the move to another small apartment at 313 West Jones, in south Phoenix. We took a Yellow Cab with our few possessions to a shed-like one-bedroom home, but I didn't see it as such. Hogans are small and cozy, so this was in my eyes another cozy space. Even my mom might have shrugged and accepted this space. The neighborhood consisted of other very small houses, apartments really, facing a courtyard with a laundry room. Any rare patches of earth beside or behind the homes were cultivated by tenants. In the back of our home was a concrete slab where my mom would later set her portable washing machine with a wringer that she filled with a hose connected to a spigot. I helped feed the clothes through the rollers of the wringer. She wrung out the jeans twice. We washed early Saturday morning before the heat became scorching. Before noon, mom unpinned our dry clothes from a clothes line my dad had erected. She must have enjoyed this new luxury because she had washed our clothes by hand when we lived in the White House.

By now my mom knew about the offenses committed at Kaibeto Boarding School. These added to her distrust of the world. On the other hand, our Navajo language was a mainstay of our belief in family solidarity. Our language stood at the door to guard against any impractical nonsense filtering into our familial space on Jones Avenue. Added to the power of our language was my mother's decision to weave. She and my dad assembled a loom and constructed weaving tools.

The sounds of her weaving made our dwelling real and transmitted a bit from our northern home.

Our new home had a living room where my brother and I played. When my mom laundered the bedding, Dean and I covered the dining table and chairs with a sheet to make a makeshift house. There we dwelled in comfortable ease—until my mom took our house covering to fold before our dad returned home. We slept on a slippery green vinyl couch with a back that unfolded to make a bed. The small kitchen was a skinny strip with a window that faced the rear of the house, where there was a space to play that couldn't exactly be called a backyard because of the absence of grass. My parents chose the rental because five blocks east of us was Rio Vista Elementary (later the school was renamed Cesar Chavez Elementary, but that was long after we moved). My dad said he and my mom wanted us to be able to walk to school. They didn't want to depend on school buses.

Once again my mom walked us to school. My brother attended first grade, and I was in second. My class door opened to a courtyard facing the third grade classrooms. We were a multicultural group of children, and in my excitement of the first day, I mistook my Latino peers for Navajo. When I discovered a girl playing tetherball by herself during lunch-recess, I broke out in Navajo.

She caught the rope under her arm. *I don't know what you're saying, but I speak Mexican.*

I decided this was only a minor barrier. *Can I play with you?*

I still stuttered when I felt uncomfortable, but if I sped through the English words, I managed to avoid speed bumps.

Monica and I played before school, during early recess, lunch-recess, and sometimes after school. I was back to play school. *Olta nanine.* I learned how to play tetherball from my Spanish-speaking friend. She was tall but was a first grader like me. We managed to play for extended periods because this tetherball was in a playground area that teachers rarely monitored. Monica and I weren't in the same class, but we hurried through whatever lunch we had so we could play. At Rio Vista, no one marched about ordering us to clean our plates. I learned to say *Thank you*, *You're welcome*, and *Please*. When an adult spoke with me, I ended our conversation with a *Thank you*. These new words had the power of Aladdin's *Open Sesame*!

My second grade teacher was Mrs. Butler, a well-dressed woman who wore suits, often a lightweight jacket with a matching skirt, always with a brooch pinned on either her left or right lapel. Her low heels clicked, announcing her arrival and where she was in the classroom. I learned to follow the clicks. She was the first person I noticed using *To our right, above our heads, behind you, before you, to your left, along the sidewalk, beside your desk*. I was still in the habit of using *Like* for confirmation: *Like this? Like that? Like where? Like now? Like when? Like why?* Mrs. Butler's prepositional phrases opened a new language of directions. I still confused right and left. The Navajo words for these were mouthfuls, and the only way I could remember which was which was by lifting my right fist and pretending to hit the tetherball. I wasn't attached to the Pledge of Allegiance, so putting my right hand over what was said to be the heart made no sense to me. Tetherball made sense.

Mrs. Butler sometimes wore dark slacks with silky printed floral blouses. Her grey brown hair was neatly curled and she wore her glasses on a lanyard. When she looked at our work, she squinted and felt for her glasses, curling up her little nose. She had crepey skin, and while she wasn't young, she had a doll like quality about her: neat, small, and efficient.

I must have disappointed her with my lack of progress, so much so that one day I was called out of class by another, much younger woman wearing high heels, exuding warmth and kindness. She instructed me to follow her.

We arrived at a small resource room where other students, mainly boys, soon poured in. Within seconds the room became a zoo. No one alighted anywhere for more than a moment or two. I sat quietly on a chair as chaos erupted around me. Students who I had seen behaved normally in the classroom or on the playground unaccountably lost control. They leaped from chairs, yelling *Look at me. I'm flying like a bird!* Countered by, *You're not a bird, stupid. Shut up, you!* I couldn't imagine what I'd done wrong to have been deposited in this place. The young teacher smiled at me and invited me into a circle. The boys continued their flying exercise.

I felt like I was in a terrible *Twilight Zone*. The noise level alone jarred my thinking. The only sounds I was accustomed to in Mrs. Butler's classroom were her wavering voice, the click of her heels, our pencil-to-paper sounds, and an occasional chair scrape or squeak. This new setting was altogether upending. Here was an environment where perfectly well-behaved kids came untethered. I didn't recognize them.

When the madness went too far, I heard my new teacher yell, *Shush!* What a breakthrough; the new teacher's use of *Shush*, a word that means bear in Navajo, confirmed what I already believed, that she secretly knew my Dine language. When I had spoken Navajo to Monica the first time we met, I was acting on the belief that everyone I was drawn to secretly spoke Navajo. The hint of annoyance that had lifted from Monica's face when we began to play tetherball was proof that she too spoke my language. Why else would she so readily accept me? I had invented and played this game of believing everyone was Navajo so often that when my new teacher called out *Shush*, I felt the hidden fall into view. My new teacher revealed her secret: she knew Navajo. Perhaps I cleaved to her single, isolated use of Navajo because I wasn't ready to start living in English language territory. My Navajo was my life, like air, water, the sun, all that I knew.

It was thus logical that I imagined a Navajo name for Monica, one that fit her. When she hit the tetherball, no matter how high I leaped, I couldn't intercept it. The mocking ball flew out of my reach as Monica posed ready to block my attempts. If I were to christen Monica, I would call her Girl-That-Hits-Hard. *At'eed ayoo adeestsii*. Assigning a name linked Monica to my life, like a kinship on some complex level, confirming that she was Navajo, but, and a big but, because of an inexplicable rule in this secret game, she unknowingly disguised her Navajo identity. She might not know it yet, but I did. If I liked a *bilagaana*, well of course, this person really is *Dine*, like me. People use all sorts of absurd illogical mind games to deal with difficult settings. I did. So when I heard my frustrated new teacher call out, *Shush!* I didn't consider the strangeness of her word choice. All I heard was the Navajo word, and all I cared about was that she really did know Navajo, just as I had suspected. Like other *bilagaanas* I was fond of, she knew Navajo but it was hidden inside. Now her secret was out. She knew my language. I instantly bonded with her.

Despite my revelatory moment, her *Shush* didn't affect the bird-boys. They continued to leap about, squawking and jeering, their behavior hovering somewhere between birds and very human, idiotic boys. All this in the presence of a too-kind young teacher and a bewildered second grader newly hearing what I thought was Navajo in the classroom. Up to this moment, I had never heard the English word *Shush*. My vocabulary was limited to *Silence, Be quiet, Sit still,* or *Shhh*, but never *Shush*. I was still gathering my English vocabulary into my small basket. Add this to the meaning of Dine, and my second grade perspective was muddled, but I wanted to bring people closer to me. In addition, I had yet to meet a Navajo educator, or even a Native-looking teacher. Later I learned that some were Native, but I was doubtful, assuming all Natives spoke their own language. Well, the real ones, at least. Forgive my small-minded thinking. I harbored these assumptions for many years.

Perhaps my long-ago first encounter with two men who clearly didn't look like my family, both trading post managers and both speakers of my language, founded my belief that all people knew Navajo. The two men were Navajo parading as *bilagaana*, white; *Nakaii*, Latino; *Nakaii lizhinii*, Black; or *Biaa'adaaalts'ozi*, Asian. The trading post managers negotiated with my grandparents, my aunts, and my mom when they sold rugs or newly sheared wool or bought groceries. I adored these moments of interaction, shopping with my eyes. If anyone complained of being lowballed, I didn't hear it. I accepted the circumstances as they were. From my second grade perspective, we were all the same. This faulty logic didn't hold water in all circumstances, but believing it allowed me to flourish at that time.

Children invent their truths to make sense of a confusing world. My brother Dean would never run home from wherever he was because he feared running home would speed up time, which would mean that he wouldn't find our mom in her rightful place in our small home. He clung to this belief no matter how many times I assured him it was impossible. *Dean, that would mean you would be older, too. Why would only Mom disappear? She'll always be home, for us.*

By this time, I had my own illogics. I had begun to see gargoyles perched on the shower wall top, but I could only see them when I looked at their reflection in the drain. In the small pool that swirled around the drain—thank God the water never stilled, for then their details might have overwhelmed the barriers that separated my world from theirs—their images were distorted, but they were indeed gargoyles. If I hadn't seen them before in a magazine, spouting from a castle wall, and asked my dad what they were, I might have called them flying demons. Yet my dad's explanation, *They guarded the occupants* and *They warded off enemies*, assuaged my fears when I saw their reflection. There were usually two of them, watching me in the shower, all jutty angles, talons, pointy ears, cheek bones, and their velvety wings folded close to their sleek bodies. They watched me. Sometimes I saw them bend down close to my head as if to sniff the odors that hot water and soap couldn't remove. Was this connected to Mr. Carrot or to the magic in which I believed? Our avid devotion to episodes of *The World Beyond* and *Twilight Zone* probably factored in as well. When our mom objected to our lying on the floor inhaling TV-land garbage, I looked to Dean's charm to break down her resolve.

To vanquish the gargoyles, I only had to turn off the shower. Confined to the resource room at school, how was I to rid myself of the bird-boys? At the close of the first session, my new teacher asked me, *Evelyn, you don't really belong in this class, do you?* I shook my head. How could bird-boys waste precious class time? I had just escaped the horrors of boarding school and found it baffling that students mocked the efforts of teachers like this one. If she or Mrs. Butler were to drop her chalk or eraser, I would no doubt have scrambled to retrieve it for them; not so for others who sat near these teachers. My mom had inspired me to exalt school and learning by reminding me that I had a very special opportunity she never had.

Before my permanent return to the classroom from the resource room, I had to take a non-text test. The same young teacher showed me a blank sheet of paper with a near-half circle at the center of the paper. She explained that I must create a drawing using that curved line. What a great assignment. I waited for her to say, *You may begin.*

I made the curve into the back of what I envisioned as a gigantic whale. I drew the blow hole with water fountaining in a shower. Beside the whale, I drew a man wearing a top hat and standing with one peg leg in a skiff. All around were endless waves. In the air, I drew elongated letter Ms for birds. I drew a smiling man waving at the smiling whale. I drew a fabulously large tail flipping a spray of water on the man.

While I was still drawing and filling in spaces with crayons, the teacher said, *Now, tell me about your picture.*

I pointed to the whale to explain. *This is Moby Dick and this is Captain Ahab. The story goes that Captain Ahab wanted to kill Moby Dick, but in this drawing I make them friends.*

I remembered Gregory Peck's ferocious eyebrows, so I quickly drew dark barbed slashes above his eyes.

My assessor nodded and asked, *Why did you choose to draw this picture?*

Because it was the only picture I could think of with this, I said, pointing at the original curve.

Can you tell me more about this story?

Ah, a challenge for my English. I warbled through enough to satisfy her.

That's when the true magic happened. I found a way out of the resource room. Never mind that I had watched the movie *Moby Dick* the previous Saturday on Channel Five KPHO's broadcast of *The World Beyond*, and that much of the language had gone right past me. Dean and I paid attention to the dramatic background music to alert us to ominous or significant events. For two partially fluent English language learners, we made the best of the special effects. Dean and I agreed that the whale looked like a wooden contraption. While I altered the story when I took my test, I rooted for Moby Dick. The whale represented mystery, the unattainable, and great power.

I hadn't told my mom about the gargoyles in the shower, which I believed would only have given them more power. As long as I avoided looking at the eerie reflections at my feet, I was fine. The gargoyles never screeched into my ears, touched me, or haunted my dreams, so I was certain they weren't as powerful as I feared. After all, I only saw them when I showered. If I happened to glance where they had once perched above the edge of the shower stall, without the water running—nothing. They weren't there. Their presentation powers were limited. Plus, while these gargoyles were clearly larger than me, they were nothing like Moby Dick, who was a powerhouse. He was gigantic, and the last image I had seen of Captain Ahab, tangled against the massive side of Moby Dick, had stayed with me. Moby Dick showed me what happens to people who pursue the impossible or the should-not.

I regained admission to Mrs. Butler's class with that single art project. Before letting me return to Mrs. Butler, the young teacher gave me some great advice that I practiced for the rest of my educational career, even in college: Pay attention, raise your hand when you know the answer, and read because it will improve your English.

Perfect advice for a dreamy, stammering student.

Once I returned to class, I was moved from the back of the room to the front, right near Mrs. Butler's desk. If she were to drop her chalk or eraser, I was in a position to come to my teacher's aid.

One day, a visitor came to our class to talk with us about Cub Scouts and Brownies. Once I got the permission form, I folded it carefully because I decided I was going to be a Brownie. I didn't understand all the details, but I knew without a doubt it was for me. Later I filled out my name, my address, my birthdate, and date, but I needed my mom's permission to stay after school for the Brownie meetings. I didn't have Dean's charm, but I could be mighty persuasive when necessary.

Earlier in the year, I told my parents I wanted boots that clacked. *Ke diset nisin.* My parents laughed, no doubt thinking that I was a strange child. My first pair were brown suede lace ups. Quite cool, but...while they indeed made the clacking sounds I liked, I didn't see many girls wearing brown boots, so I asked for another pair. This time my mom gave me soft shiny vinyl black boots with a respectable heel and an inside zipper. About this same time, my mom made me a hot pink print sleeveless drop-waist dress with a flared bottom. I twirled a lot when I wore this dress, not exactly what my mom had in mind when she made it. When I wore it, with yellow netted tights, the crosswalk lady observed, *My, you look very pretty today.* I hadn't heard those words much, if at all, so I appreciated the moment. Was it worth getting dolled up to hear such praise? I wasn't sure. I liked the effect but not the process.

For picture day, my mom had curled my hair in sausage curls, then tied it in ponytails embellished with fuzzy yellow ribbon. Quite amazing since many compared my hair to goat hair. It was fine, straight, and had taken Herculean efforts to produce the Nellie Oleson look. That was the compromise: if I wanted the knee high boots, I would have to accept being primped by my mom.

I was prepared for all manner of beautifying so that I could become a Brownie. My mom loved nothing more than my docile acquiescence as she played with my hair. About this same time, she bought me a brown leather purse with a long strap. I used to bury my nose in the leather because its musky scent made me think of other pleasures: the smell of a freshly waxed saddle; new shoes; a leather vest with fringes that my mom wore with her jeans and boots. Unwilling or unable to mimic my mother's feminine way of placing the long strap delicately on her shoulder, I resorted to swinging the purse like a Scottish athlete competing in a hammer throw, hitting anything that entered my path, mainly family members. Round and round I went, gaining momentum, and using all the power I had in my arms and back to swing my beautiful brown friend. Once, waiting at a bus stop with my mom on Central Avenue, I wondered wickedly how my purse would fare if I hit a passing vehicle with it. It's safe to say that my mom retired that missile of a purse, stowing it high up in the closet, *You can't take care of nice things*, roughly translated from *doo baa'aholyadah*. I didn't want to think I was proving to be a disappointment, at least in the realm of more conventional beauty like hers, but it did surface as a possibility.

Once I had talked my mom into permitting me to attend the Brownie troop meeting, I waited for the meeting date. I learned the magic words: *I'll learn a lot, I'll be good*, and *I'll come home as soon as the meeting is over*. The meeting was all that I imagined: I was welcomed, made to feel valued, and was given *refreshments*—another new word. We had cookies and lemonade. After our treats, we played very polite games, nothing at all like tetherball or slinging projectiles. Everything was pleasantly tame: my peers, our teacher, and the games.

Our Brownie troop leader, a teacher who worked at Rio Vista Elementary, displayed the uniform that identified Brownie-hood for us, and showed us the badges we would earn by fulfilling Brownie duties, projects, and expectations. I felt I was part of a greater whole. My family had built a foundation, but I sought more social identity-bearing recognition. Several meetings had passed when our troop leader announced she needed our uniform fees. I had the good sense to know my parents wouldn't whip open a wallet for this. On a weekend visit to a thrift store on south Central Avenue, I happened upon used Brownie uniforms on the racks. I found one I thought would fit me, but then saw other uniforms with badges pinned to them. I would be one step ahead of the game. I removed all the badges from the other uniforms and pinned them on what would soon be mine. Later, when my mom bought the uniform, the cashier winked at me. I felt she knew and approved of my cunning. I compared switching Brownie badges to crossing a field diagonally instead of walking around it, working on homework early so I would have less at home, flipping to the harder math problems to try them out before doing the simpler ones, or sneaking a look at a book's ending if the plot knotted my belly into tangled balls of stress.

When I wore my regalia to school on the day of the next Brownie meeting, I sported all the badges that I had reattached after my mom laundered my brand-new used uniform. At the meeting itself, my troop leader quietly removed every pin. *We'll save these for your achievements, Evelyn.* I didn't feel wounded or even gently chided. Instead I felt I had helped her somehow. I amassed more badges for her.

In Mrs. Butler's class there was a boy who was as short as I was. He had curly hair and thick brown plastic glasses, and when he really concentrated, his mouth opened a bit as if to inhale the information, unlike those of us who needed to use our eyes to read or study. While others raised their hands patiently and routinely to affirm Mrs. Butler's instruction, Denny Garcia just asked his questions. She prized his questions, which propelled her lessons forward. I also liked Denny's wonderings. He often asked questions that were already whirling in my head. I still hesitated to say anything, but I remained attentive, just as I had been advised by the resource teacher. Watching Denny, who was guided by his own curiosity, and observing the way his mouth formed such smooth strings of words, my first crush formed. As luck would have it, he didn't know I existed. However, we often were paired as walking partners. Sometimes when I heard Mrs. Butler say, *Boys and girls, hold hands as we walk to the library*, I reached for Denny's sweaty soft hand before she finished her sentence. If his damp grip slackened in mine, I held on. Undaunted by disinterest, I loved Denny with all my second-grade heart. That said, my love burned brightest in the classroom. At recess, my fantastic energy superseded even love, and the idea of playing with Denny never occurred to me.

Once at home, with my homework done, if I had free time between playtime and dinner, I conjured Denny in fragmented, vivid snatches. Sometimes I composed love notes that I never gave him, missives that were more magical in my head than on paper. The wonder of my first love was in reverie—daydreaming about Denny when I was away from him or drawing his face on notebook paper. Despite holding his hand in line at school or on an occasional field trip, my Denny love was the figurative kind. I admired his thick glasses, his nasal voice, his brown curly uncombed hair. He was disheveled but nice to everyone, even to me tugging on him as we walked in pairs. I wrote Denny's name in hidden places, and traced the letters of his name on the couch as I drifted off to sleep. I even created a name search game as I walked to school. I searched for the letter D on a license plate, then E and when I saw an N I counted it as two. If I had difficulty with Y, I cheated. I used the Y in my name to spell his. By the time I spelled his first name, I had lost interest in the game.

I learned from this crush that affection flowing one way can be a thoroughly enjoyable experience. What could I do beyond what I had felt and done? I couldn't imagine. I already knew the powerlessness of childhood. My mom kept me out of her kitchen when she prepared meals, she gave me a purse that she then took away from me, I wore dresses when I wanted to wear pants, and recess always ended far too soon. A crush seemed to fall into this category: more desire than fulfillment.

My interest in writing brief love letters to Denny was in part an intense interest in letter writing itself. I was aware that my dad received letters from his home. I decided to write to my cousin-sister Venne. I used notebook paper. The beginning was easy. *Dear Fannie.* I used her formal name. I wrote the standard *How are you?* I added *I am well.* Then because I was getting stuck already, I added *My family is well. They all say hello.* Now that the formality was over, I would talk about school, the only real news I had. *Dean and I are gun*—I stopped here because I wanted to write *gonna*, but I wasn't sure how to spell it. When I pronounced *gonna*, I heard a short /u/ sound. My family had left the Bible story set at the White House, but in Phoenix we had a dictionary and a thesaurus, Dean's and my library books from school, and a few issues of *National Geographic* issues, our version of coffee table picture books. We didn't drink coffee, but we did have a low table in front of the couch where I propped myself on my knees as I did my homework or read my library books. Now I used the age old strategy of looking up my word in the dictionary by sounding it out. I looked up G, but when I added the /u/ I heard, I landed on the word *gun*. The word I fully expected to see soon after was *guna* just as I pronounced it. No matter how many times I started, no word was listed, so I tried G followed by an /o/. There again, no luck.

By now any urgency in writing my letter had dissolved, and I was on a word hunt. It was another gargoyle moment: How can this be? I was annoyed because I already had my doubts about the worth of the English language. At a time when I knew more Navajo, I couldn't understand how this inferior language—English—could trump Navajo. I valued the wit and ingenuity of my mother tongue.

In English, we say *Give it to me*. There's no telling what the *it* is unless it's been stated previously. In my language, the *it* is precise. If the item is a blanket, the *it* shows that whatever is desired will require a two-handed delivery in terms of weight, such as a blanket that has flexible mass. The same is true if the *it* is a tool like a jack. Then the *it* indicates a solid object. True too of newspaper. The fluttery light quality would be denoted in the *it*. My mother tongue also had a poetic quality that imbued it with wit. Once my uncle described his carburetor trouble as a coughing vehicle. We smiled when he described it, but it also gave his vehicle an animate quality. A listener would have compassion for the vehicle and the speaker because the connotation would unify the pair. Truck and driver are dependent on one another. Such attention to the *it* implied that inanimate objects deserved respect. Objects weren't simply there for our casual, haphazard use, but were in our lives for a reason. There was a relationship to be had. Once again the *take care* phrase resurfaced with greater meaning for me: *baa aholya*. By second grade, I knew I needed to take care of my language, *saad*. The sentence *ni saad baa aholya* was a constant reminder of the holiness of my language because thoughts preceded my words. My mom added thoughts, too, so I knew of my accountability to the spirit of my words. Every stuttered word, a great annoyance in rushed moments, was the projection of my *iina*, my air spirit. My writing deserved equal reverence.

    Here I was, at a standstill before a word I thought I had mastered. My dad wouldn't be home for hours. My mom was no closer to speaking English than in the past. My little brother was useless.

    I had an unwavering belief that every day was designed specifically for me. If I found a penny, I was the person who was destined to find it, and I proffered my *Thank you* as I pocketed it. I had the same approach to people I met or befriended. The world was indeed wonderful. Yes, I experienced unfairness, but I experienced it as a challenge. I folded my letter and took my pencil to my friend's house, kitty-corner to ours. After I knocked, she came to the door and I asked if I could speak to her older sister.

Somewhere I had retained a memory of my El Monte friend-neighbor-schoolmate Becky's older sister who had helped us learn to tie our shoelaces. She listened as I shared my dictionary impasse with *guna*, and gave it to me straight: *Gonna isn't a real word. You won't find it in the dictionary.* Hearing this was like climbing a long, steep, circuitous flight of stairs, then reaching a landing with no door and nowhere to go. What I thought was English was not. How great this disappointment was. What I assumed was solid ground was as insubstantial as mist. Initially bewildered, I angrily blamed everyone from my teachers to my friends for allowing me to use *gonna*. I was unhappiest with my teachers, whose betrayal I felt keenly. In their presence they had let me use this word repeatedly, never once correcting my usage.

Seeing the disappointment playing on my face, my friend's older sister came to my rescue. *Use will instead.* What hope in four letters. Of course. I thanked her and returned to my letter-writing, slightly less enthusiastic but much more knowledgeable about the discovered limits of my English language.

This experience launched my letter writing habit. I wrote to cousins and to my grandmother Lucy. My mom had finally found a useful task for me: I became her personal correspondent. Standing in the kitchen preparing her signature delectables, she dictated until I balked: *I can't write that fast!* or *I don't know how to say that in English.* She might have harbored doubts about some junctures in my education, but in this situation, I met her expectations. Translation took time, but I worked hard. If I took too long to translate, the moment was gone and a new topic was at hand. When I finished a letter, she surveyed my writing. *You have to write your name, Shima. Here.* I pointed to the space at the bottom.

She never stopped until both sides of the paper were filled, exercising frugality even in letter writing, so I had to run back and forth into her domain, the kitchen, to show her my progress on paper. She signed the letter and then handed me an envelope to fill out. Here again, I used my main foolproof strategy: I copied patterns from letters we received. Initially I made the mistake of writing the recipient's address in the return section of the envelope and wrote my mom's name and address as the recipient. Needless to say, we figured out my mistake when the letter was delivered back to us. I never made that error again.

Dean must have observed my letter-writing duties with interest because he suggested that we write to the KPHO hosts of *The Wallace and Ladmo Show*. *We can draw Gerald and get our Ladmo bags sent to us*, he suggested. As an initiate of the Hall of Fame of Imbecilic Optimism, I wondered why I hadn't thought of this before. Of course we would win the coveted Ladmo bags. To save ourselves the trip to the television studio, we'd have them send our Ladmo bags to 313 West Jones. The prize was a given because Dean and I were natural artists. What a plan. We got to be mean to Gerald and win a bag of prizes besides. Brilliant.

So began our letter-drawing campaign to *The Wallace and Ladmo Show*. We gave up only after writing for several years, but during the time we had hope on our side, we had a great time designing mean Gerald art. We watched with the hope that one magnificent morning our names would be announced and our art would be shown to viewers of the Greater Phoenix area and any other communities that received the seven o'clock morning children's broadcast. Nope, not even a postcard apologizing that Ladmo bags could not be mailed. It probably didn't help that we always wrote *Please send us our Ladmo bags*. My brother, his mean spirit surfacing, drew Gerald in hapless situations. One featured poor Gerald sitting on his throne with Ladmo standing nearby covering his mouth as Gerald has a bowel movement. Dean drew actual plump, very plump, fecal matter charging through the sewer pipes. I don't recall what I drew, but it never matched the meanest of mean. I doubt that I ever topped his artistry.

My parents must have thought we had reached the age of accountability and responsibility because they began leaving us by ourselves in the evening. We never had a babysitter. We really didn't know what that meant. In our mom's eyes, it meant having an uninvited visitor in our home. To compensate, when they left us alone, our dad commanded that the

Chapter 3 - Second Grade: Moby Dick

front door be locked at all times, not opened for anyone. My dad tested us on following directions by having us practice locking the front door while he stood outside. He proceeded to knock and tell us to open up, which we promptly did. He reentered, wagging his finger at us. *We said to keep the door locked at all times*! Even in second grade, I knew they shouldn't have left us alone in a questionable neighborhood late into the night. My parents left and sometimes didn't return until well past our bedtimes.

Once or twice, our parents did catch us watching TV as we drowsily camped out, but in those days TV-land offered limited viewing pleasure options. Certainly not enough to keep us glued to it. Everyone knew the best TV was in the morning, especially Saturday mornings. There were five channels, Channel Five, our beloved KPHO; Channel Eight, KAET, the artsy public channel with *Evening at the Pops*; Channel 10, CBS; Channel 12, NBC; Channel 3, ABC; and a very snowy Channel 45 that we resorted to listening to instead of watching. I think our mom felt a tinge of guilt for abandoning us. She always made us a wonderful dinner for us, so we were never underfed on the evenings of their escape.

Once they were gone, and we had waited long enough, my brother and I ventured out the back door. We kept the front door locked as instructed by our parents, but they had never said anything about the back door. Dean went looking for his friends, and I rode my bike.

The previous summer, my dad had borrowed a relative's bike to teach me how to ride on our sandy, sun-baked dirt roads at the White House. My dad had held the tail of the banana seat as he trotted behind me. I hadn't yet figured out that a firm grasp was key to not steering wildly. I crashed often. For all the cactus lining the dirt roads, I never once fell into a prickly pear. That was for later.

Dad, wait! You're going too fast. Stop! I yelled once. But I heard his laughter fading and realized he wasn't pushing me. I was pedaling myself, heading to my *Nali Sani*'s house. I rode proudly around her house, but when I tried to turn my bike back to where my dad waited, I wobbled and came to a weaving, tottering crash.

My dad hadn't taught me how to stop the bike. I learned to crash stop, getting up with cuts, scrapes, and bruises growing on top of previous bruises, but the speed was so glorious I got back on the bike again and again. The bike was too high for me, and I couldn't position it upright, so I always set out from an incline, using my momentum to begin pedaling. The sheer power of speed, the sense of freedom from the tickle of invisible debris charging into my face, arms, and legs and the wind whipping my hair was nothing short of amazing.

The brand new bike my folks brought me was my horse. My steed. My steed friend who knew me and knew my heart. I liked how I rode curves and turns at a daring angle. I defied gravity and rode crazy fast. Such power. I still had an occasional crash, but it was well-worth it for the speed. When my neighborhood friends asked to ride my bike, I made sure they rode out of sight of our mom's constant supervision. Despite leaving my brother and me alone most weekend evenings, our mom watched us like a hawk when we played in the neighborhood. However, I had developed another non-logic to accommodate that contradiction: I believed that my mom had the power to read my thoughts (lying to her was futile), and the power to keep me safe.

Of my very few bicycle-related challenges, one was the occasional flat tire. My dad quietly patched my tire. He placed my bike upside down and secured one side as he unscrewed the nut. He removed the washer and then the tire. He flattened the tire by using a pin to release more air, then removed the inner tube from between the rim and tire. In a small container of water, he searched for the hole by rotating it by inches while submerged. Once he found the puncture, he rubbed it with a small file to roughen the area for the patch. I eventually learned to make my own repairs, adding to my liberation.

Dean also had a bike his height, but he could ride only a little more than half a block before the chain fell from the sprocket and we had to turn the bike upside down to fit the chain back in the groove. We did this repeatedly, never thinking to complain. It was simply a feature of Dean's bike. It wasn't long before he wanted to share my bike. Again, this drew no complaint. Only 18 months apart, we were used to sharing without squabbling.

Near this time, my dad brought home a 1960 beige Chevrolet truck with exterior tire hubs and a narrow platform in front of the hubs where I imagined I'd stand as he drove. The bed of the truck was oiled wood reinforced with metal rods.

In the Phoenix heat, getting in shoeless was asking for burnt and splintered soles. The cab fit all of us with plenty of room.

My dad proudly displayed his used-but-new vehicle. He didn't tell my mom how much he had withdrawn from her savings to buy his first vehicle. My mom wasn't happy, but she grew to accept it. More than once, I watched my dad pull into a gas station, say, *Fill'er up*, and when the attendant asked for payment, Dad looked at Mom. She unclasped her purse to fish out the funds.

While she was used to seeing my dad spend his whole paycheck, she managed to save her earnings from rug sales. My mom continued to weave rug after rug. Where she sold them all remains a mystery to me. If she earned a dollar, she would subtract a quarter for savings. She believed that money should be protected and controlled, like Dean and me.

Though my dad couldn't save, he managed to buy my mom a washing machine with a hand-turning wringer. Before that, my mom had walked our laundry to a laundromat off Central Avenue. One afternoon, in a hurry, she loaded clothes into a dryer without shaking out the clothing first. Later when she unloaded the dried clothes, she found what she thought was a sturdy green cigarette. It turned out to be a rolled up one-hundred-dollar bill. Shortly after that, my mom made the mistake of telling my dad how she paid for the great home-prepared steak meal we all enjoyed. Fortunately, she had safely deposited the remainder of the hundred dollars but my dad practiced the age-old Navajo what's-yours-is-mine-and-what's-mine-is-yours prerogative.

Since he had learned about her savings, my dad had persisted in trying to persuade my mom to add his name to her account. In my mom's eyes, my dad mismanaged the funds from his high-paying job. To her, any job was high paying because she appreciated the value of work and savings. To her, work was a privilege. Eventually my mom's savings had grown into a respectable sum that my dad, a non-saver, viewed as an opportunity to spend. He had convinced her that he should have equal access to the benefits of her hard labor. It wasn't long before she checked her balance while depositing some funds and discovered it was drained dry. Happy with his new truck purchase, my dad didn't ask about their shared account again. He knew he had depleted it. She closed that account and opened another with a small deposit. She hid her deposit book. But thanks to my mom's thrift and discipline, my family had its first vehicle. I imagine my dad felt that same freedom in his beige truck that I did when I rode my bike around the neighborhood.

During one of our parents' evening escapades in the 1960 Chevrolet, my brother and I slipped out the back door as usual. After our fun and games, we returned through the same back door but we sensed something was not as it should be. Everything was in place, and if we stood where the dining table was, we could see into the bedroom and part of the bathroom. The bathroom door was ajar. Recalling the gargoyles, I imagined that they had escaped the bathroom. I accepted the fact that gargoyles had flown from their usual perch on the shower stall wall. This night, we spied an upright shadow in our parents' bedroom. We thought our mom or dad had unexpectedly returned while we were out playing. The family truck often had a flat tire or needed repairs. We checked in front of the house, but no truck. But someone was definitely in the bedroom. All we could make out was a vertical shadow that lingered in the darkened bedroom.

Shima? Silence.

Dad? Silence.

We didn't have the courage to clasp hands and step into our parents' bedroom. We hurried to a friend's house to report that someone was in our house. We must have created a stir because no one wanted to investigate. When the well-meaning parents of our friend invited us to stay with them until our parents returned, we suspected we would have a hard time explaining that situation, so we returned to our backyard.

We waited while the daylight faded. The city street lamps deepened from tepid yellow to bright amber. We heard the cicadas humming, dogs barking in the dark, and moths flapping against the bare light bulb above the back door. The light bulb buzzed and the glare was alive with moths' wings batting at the surface. When one too many cockroaches ran for our feet, we relented and entered the silent house. I flicked on the kitchen light. Dean hugged close to me; moving as one, we turned on the TV, then we peeked into the shadowy darkness of our parents' bedroom. Whatever was there before had relocated. The heavy prickly atmosphere cleared, returning our small home to us. The walls and furniture invited us back to our space.

I grew from this experience. I learned space had dimensions. If a place has no human activity or is left alone, as we had done when we'd left the house to itself, the space changes, inviting others, that palpable presence that's always visible to everyone. I knew we had to claim and enliven our space somehow, so when my parents happened to be out, I stayed inside the apartment house while Dean sought the company of his friends. I occupied my time with drawing, writing, and reading. I also spent much of the time lost in daydreams. Without doubt, I knew my life held unknown promises. I knew not what they were, but they were and would stay wonderful. I was so sure. I certainly didn't want to interfere with those promises by opening the wrong door or tripping before reaching and opening my proper door. The game show *Let's Make a Deal* might have played into this theorizing.

My brother and I were still young enough to accompany one another when one of us needed to use the toilet, wash our hands before dinner, or wash up after playing outside. Our mom never let us forget the privilege of modern plumbing. Not flushing the toilet elicited my mom's worst tirades, but sometimes hearing that chortle retort of flushing scared us, causing us to scuttle away. All we got from our very unsympathetic dad was a dry, *Listen to your mom.*

Now that he was working and providing for our family, my dad had returned to referring to our mom as *homemaker* or *housewife*. He was a proud earner even though he had holes in his financial management. He may not have been able to save a dime, but he had married a smart, frugal partner. She could turn gunnysacks full of oily sheep wool into finely colored, tightly-woven rugs. And every night, she cooked delicious meals out of the meager grocery money my dad allotted her. Tightfisted, he gave my mom only a few dollars, but he wanted to eat like a king.

Our dad also suffered from Peter Pan syndrome. Though Dean and I were school-aged and our dad had a loyal wife, he still wanted to play the field. He may have suffered from the *Yahz* syndrome found in some Navajo families: the son is given every privilege, and he exercises no self-control, all his whims satisfied by his parents—principally his mom. Or he might have had an ungenerous mother, my *Nali*, who withheld affection, so he sought that affection from other women. His need for approval may have been so great that he risked family, security, love, health, and STDs. On the plus side, my dad's man-child behavior led to swimming at the public pool, relaxing on blankets in a public park while snacking on Doritos and bean dip with a Coke, and having Saturday cookouts at South Mountain Park when he was home. The minus side involved waiting for him to return home on payday, then finally seeing him Saturday evening or Sunday morning with reddened, watery eyes and purplish bruises on his neck. When I first saw my dad this way, I was terrified, worrying that someone had tried to choke him. I didn't help his cause when I cried loudly, calling my mom's attention to those marks. I waited for an answer to my mom's question.

Who chewed your neck? Haisha nizagi yi yii aal?

But my dad waved me away, laughing in a strained way. I recall him digging into the meal my mom had cooked earlier and saved for whatever hour he returned. It seemed much too easy for him to take advantage of my mom's generosity. Because he assigned my mom the role of housewife, he expected her to be responsible for our rearing, our school and home conduct, and our well-being. His responsibility ended as soon as he found an apartment within walking distance from the public school. That's why he always asked *How were the kids?* when he arrived home from work. If he needed to spank us, he relied on my mom's direction because once he showered, he wholly expected the benefits of being with well-behaved children.

Every once in a while something happened that confirmed my theory that mine would be a wonderful life. A landmark event was our class field trip to the Phoenix Orpheum Theatre to watch the play *Pinocchio*. I got my mom's signature on the permission form. By now, though my mom couldn't read or write, she knew how to sign her name with a flourish. She did this for the letters I wrote for her as well as the occasional note from my teacher Mrs. Butler that required an acknowledgment. Report cards, too, had to be signed by parents and returned. I never brought home any recriminating notes from my teacher, thanks I'm sure, to the timely advice of my short-term resource teacher. Dean, by contrast, came home with notes pinned to his shirt with straight pins that basically said: *I didn't pay attention in class today*. My mom couldn't read it, but she gave it to our dad. Dean was belted for that. While I might have harbored odd, unfounded beliefs about my future adult life, he clearly was a person of the moment. He sought joy without patience. However, Dean had an amazing amount of charm that won everyone over. By the time his teacher wrote that occasional misbehavior note, I'm sure she had given him generous chances. His mere smile undid my mom, friends, and teachers and other adults, and even me.

My mom also started the practice of correcting my brother's and my pigeon-toed walk. She stuck masking tape on the short hallway from the dining table to the west wall. I quickly figured out that I had to step straight forward without losing my balance and even bragged to my mom that I could run with my feet pointed straight. Poor Dean couldn't. More whacks on his butt for that. I played outside while he was sentenced to walk until my mom was satisfied he showed improvements.

While some might have viewed these corrections as punitive, I saw them as small lessons that added up to some vague greater good. My mom was preparing Dean and me for public experiences.

So was Mrs. Butler. She prepared our class for *Pinocchio*. On the special Orpheum Theatre day, I was dressed in my best, thanks to my mom, who had also dampened a rag to wipe the dust from my boots. My hair was Aqua-netted in place, stiff and motionless, but I knew my hair and shoes met my mom's approval. At school, we double-filed with our usual partner (Denny!) out to the school bus that transported us downtown. Prior to this, as with Mom's military-like supervision of our steps, Mrs. Butler gave us lots of *Boys-and-girls-in-the-theatre-we-will* talks. We learned we would single file into the theatre and leave no empty seats between us. We would walk in quietly, sit quietly, and enjoy the play, quietly and when it was over, clap politely, as she had demonstrated. While some boys made silly faces as they clapped their fingers against their curled palms and lifted their noses in the air, I studied to make sure I mimicked her new high society clap. I wanted to get it right. Like my mom, Mrs. Butler wanted to be proud of us. For added measure, I stepped with my toes straight in front of me without losing my balance.

The theater seat cushioned my bottom and I rested my arms on the armrests, but the seat was meant for a much larger person and had far more space than I could fill. My feet didn't touch the floor. I studied the heavy velvet drapes that covered the mysterious stage. How I wanted to know what was behind the stage. For the first time, I experienced the collective anticipation shared by millions before and since when seated, programs in hand, before the maroon curtain and its mystery. This wasn't like the introductory music that announced the upcoming program. This was huge, exponentially bigger than sitting before a small TV screen. Any knowledge about Pinocchio, its characters, good and bad, was dwarfed by the setting, which enveloped me, my class, and everyone in the theater. Mrs. Butler looked even smaller and more doll-like than in the classroom. She sat near the other end of the row as she hushed those around her. I didn't need any reminders of proper theater behavior. I was entranced and awed by everything.

I was also taken back to my *Nali Sani*'s small safe abode where the green broadcloth had been made into a humble curtain tied to a tacked nail. I felt the same safety and coziness but with the unbelievable joy of high anticipation. This giddiness was new for me, but it reminded me of times in El Monte listening to my dad read Bible stories with strange names and constant references to God. I was easily impressed, but this was far beyond any dream. I wouldn't go to a real movie theater until much later, but when I did, it would not match the splendor of the Orpheum. Not even close. I felt like I was in the presence of godliness, like I was a Moses standing before a burning bush waiting for God to inscribe the Ten Commandments. I felt I had stepped into a realm of the holy of holies.

I don't know if we had a live orchestra, but the sound was stereo before stereo as most know it. Our class was situated in the back row of the first level. When the play began, I tipped back because the sound seemed to vibrate through my core. When I saw the Blue Fairy suspended in the air, I ignored the harness wire. If there was intermission, I stayed where I was, glued to my seat. *Pinocchio* seemed to have halted all of my body systems except my breathing. I fell under its spell. I saw myself as the main character, wanting the all of life, the hard to reach, and the impossible. And I wanted to be good even though I had almost fallen into the clutches of the Jacks of life. Yet, I also knew Blue Fairies existed to give redemption and sway the unknown gods that observed my struggles. I was indeed Pinocchio.

When we came out from the darkened theater and our eyes adjusted, nothing prepared me for the blinding light of the sun. In my appreciation of the theatre, I imagined what a baby must feel receiving the jarring upset of birth—shuddering at the sudden blare of sound, movement, and environment. I felt a rebirth of sorts. Whatever that experience was, I decided I wanted more and more of it.

CHAPTER 4
Third Grade: Two Different Teachers

My second grade year ended. My mom wanted to get her driver's license. My parents left us early Saturday mornings for my mom's driving lessons with my dad, who promised us a park pool visit when they returned. Always a quick learner, my mom became a skilled driver with minimal input from my dad. No doubt my dad would have been happy to have been her teacher for longer, modeling his masculine know-how, but the lessons were over nearly as soon as they started. The next step was the written portion of the driving test. Because my mom could not read, write, or speak English, she needed a Navajo translator for that part. One of the few places to accommodate drivers-to-be like my mom was the Department of Motor Vehicles north of Page, Arizona, close to the Utah state line.

The day we drove to the DMV in Page was a sunny day in June 1972, nowhere near a Phoenix-broil. I wore another lime green dress sewn by my mom in that ever-hopeful color from a bolt of fabric at a store on Central Avenue. She sewed two white candy-like buttons to the front of the waistband. The sun on my bare arms and legs with the wind blowing my hair into a matted mess was the best thing about riding in the back of the pickup. My mom had placed a sturdy mat in the bed of the truck to cover the metal and wooden floor boards so Dean and I would be comfortable. In addition, she sewed covers with thick foam sitting pads for us. Well before seatbelt laws, this was how many Navajo families traveled to town for laundry, groceries, and have-to-get-to-town plans. This time we drove north, past second windmill, past my Uncle Jerry's Baptist Church, past the Coppermine Trading Post turnoff and a rise of cedars before descending into Page, my birthplace.

Although my mom could now drive a stick shift so that the vehicle purred under her touch, her written driving test was not as smoothly navigated. My dad, who acted as her translator during that test, maintained that he provided some assistance by marking a few answers for my mom. He shared this story with us whenever our mom was ready to drive. He made a wickedly frightened face when she was at the wheel. The truth is I felt safer when she was driving us than when he did.

Despite my father's story, my mother passed her driving test that day, and we marked the occasion by stopping at the Glen Canyon Dam, near Page, where my brother and I had been born. My parents had lived in a small trailer, their first experience of independence from the firm grip of their parents and families.

Glen Canyon Dam was a place of magnificent beauty. The sandstone reds contrasted with liquid blues. While my parents walked ahead musing over the gigantic dam structure, the canyon reds, and the immense blues of Lake Powell, I scampered on the protective wall beside the path so I could peer down at the blue-green lake adjacent to the dam. Directly below me, I saw a car and a truck on a narrow track of road that appeared to be built into the north side of the dam. Leaning over the guardrail, I marveled at how small these ordinarily large car bodies looked from the height of the guard wall. Then I saw two light-colored fish in the lake far below the track of road. They were resting in the depth of the lake, and as the water's surface shimmered, I was mesmerized by their outlines and their tails waving gently. I even saw what I thought were whiskers, like those of catfish.

The fish looked so peaceful at rest in the water. Just then I happened to see one of the two vehicles move. I observed that the fish remained where they were, still at rest. That's when horror touched my belly, as I realized that if I could see two large fish in the water as clearly as the vehicles below, these fish must be greater in size than the vehicles because the water was farther away. I had a sickening thought about the mighty dimensions of the two fish that by now had swum out of my sight, farther north. When I first glimpsed the fish, I had marveled at their beauty and peacefulness, but now I became fixated by their massive size. I had a hard time believing what I saw. Saying I *saw two fishes by the dam* didn't do them justice, but saying I *saw two monster fishes* sounded unbelievable. Even when I ran the statement through my head, rehearsing it, I sounded ridiculous.

I was already familiar with the story of Jonah and the whale, but that was in a book. At my age, books had that wonderful fairy-tale quality, and the story ended once I closed the book's covers. Added to that, Jonah's whale was a story in an ancient book, and I already had a growing suspicion about the truthfulness of biblical stories. They reminded me of Coyote stories. Clearly Coyote was a teacher of sorts, a foolhardy instructor warning the more foolhardy. Losing his eyes in one story and then scattering stars to make the Milky Way in another. Well, or so it goes.

Unlike characters in books, this was the first time I had seen living creatures this enormous with my own eyes. I vacillated between seeing Jonah's whale and Moby Dick as entertainment and warning. What the warnings were I couldn't verbalize or piece together, but I felt them in my core. This led me to recall the spectacular reflection of gargoyles in our shower stall. I had by this time learned that gargoyles were posted on the high walls of castles and were designed to frighten, like mean dogs in a yard but on a greater scale. Now that I had witnessed the massive size of the two fish in broad daylight, I could no longer dismiss the gargoyles so easily. Added to this, I knew the power of corn pollen, songs, prayers, and even my favorite socks. I looked towards the northern sections of Lake Powell where I imagined the two fish might have swum, and where boaters and water skiers were visible. Rather uncomfortably, I wondered if any of them saw what I saw, the huge fish that roamed in pairs in the great depths of this inviting lake.

When my parents called for me, I slid down the rail guard with relief, hurrying to join the normal-sized world that was so familiar to me.

While my dad drove us home to the White House from Phoenix; however, my mom drove Dean and me and anyone who wanted to join us, from the White House to her parents' home. My dad kept his polite distance from his in-laws. In Phoenix, I ordinarily dallied on weekends, but when I knew we were going to my maternal grandparents' house, I never failed to rise early and declare a winning battle with my hair by brushing and braiding it. My grandmother occupied a special place in my heart. She was the *it* of my life. She seemed to embody the square root of all that was good in life: my thoughts; my imagination; the strength in my body, of which I was becoming aware; my mom; my brother; and the people I loved. When my mom criticized me in front of her mother, my grandmother held my hand and looked from my mom to me as she laughed at my mom's depictions. When I lay my head in her lap, I saw her hooked nose and smile. I sometimes traced my nose to feel for the bump, like hers.

When we first arrived at their home in the new beige truck, my grandparents came out, to admire it. *I wove many rugs for this*, my mom explained. My *Cheii* surveyed the exterior, and my mom opened the nose, what most call the hood, for him to inspect. He whistled his admiration. My mom had grown up using a wooden wagon, *tsinaabaas*, for hauling wood and water, so vehicles were new in our family. Like everyone, we remarked on so-and-so's pickup, a source of envy and pride. The evidence of social advancement was the purchase of a new truck. The opposite was awful: the loss of a truck imputed a decline in a family's economic circumstances.

My grandparents' youngest daughter, my Aunt Dorothy, was still a teen then. She, like my mom, never attended school. I wonder if the boarding school stories were notorious by the time she was school age, but she was also the baby of the family. She was wonderful company, a young version of my happy *Ma Sani*. Like *Ma Sani*, she appreciated us. She had a laugh like the peals of a bell.

Aunt Dorothy made us forts where she cooked bread and made us vehicles out of wooden planks and dirt that we pretended to drive. She made our visits all about play. She let me sit behind her on a saddled horse. My grandmother always decided which horse was best because like my mom, my Aunt Dorothy liked reckless speeds, and being bucked off was all part of the fun of horseback riding. Sometimes she rode bareback. She was the tough Pippi Longstocking from books. My grandmother, knowing her daughter well, chose gentle rides when I rode with my Aunt Dorothy. Dorothy had thick jet black hair that seemed blue sometimes. She was strong, and she saddled the horse easily as she told us a joke or story. My mom loved her littlest sister, so we followed in suit, but Dorothy was naturally easy to love.

Dorothy was born well after the end of my grandparents' wilder days and after most of their children were already parents. In fact, she was younger than some of her nieces and nephews. My dear aunt was pampered, treated like the final blessing bestowed upon older parents. My *Ma Sani* said *Do-thee*, (her pronunciation), was the only child of hers born in a hospital. She added that it was in the hospital that she had succumbed to mild labor sleepiness. When the nurse came to check on her, she was shocked to see Dorothy had been born while my *Ma sani* slept. The nurse observed small movements under the sheet, and when she lifted the covering, there was my tiny Aunt Dorothy. My *Ma Sani* smiled as she related this to me, but I was stunned to learn that baby-having was the same as animal birthing. My great love of animals far surpassed my love of people. If I saw a person with a dog, I naturally paid more attention to the furry creature-person. I studied the animal carefully, how it held its head, the position and movements of its tail or ears, how perfectly still it stood or how it pulled toward me, wanting to sniff me to confirm its impressions. I mentally sent messages introducing myself. If the dog was closer to puppyhood, that was even better.

    I already knew a little something about animal birthing. I knew about the suctioning sound of birth, the agitation of a mother-to-be, and the slippery wetness of the newly born. Now that I had heard how my Aunt Dorothy was born, I acknowledged that perhaps people birthing could hold a magic like that of animals. Maybe. While I looked at any birthing, now even those of babies like my Aunt Dorothy, with a combination of reverence, discomfort, and a big dose of wonder, for me puppies and lambs remained the celestials of babyhood.

When we arrived at my grandmother's, we went to the sheep corral since we had arrived before they were released to pasture. I stood beside my grandmother as she and my mom gazed at the herd. The corral was made from the trunks of cedar trees, hewed down by axes. This corral was old, constructed before my grandparents had a chainsaw, another important claim in Navajo economics. I don't know who helped, but I figured my tall, strong uncles chopped the trees, stripped the stringy bark and hauled them using a wagon or two. That's only the beginning; digging holes for the tree trunks would have spelled additional long days of labor. These were planted in a circular vertical wall like a hogan but without a roof. Despite being open to the elements, the sheep corral always felt warm to me, even on snowy days. The collective body of sheep nestled against the wind in a huddled mass made me feel safe. And despite the age of the corral, I could still catch the faint scent of cedar when I peeked through the cracks in between the wooden poles. Still, the overall smell was sheep dung, deep green pellets that broke as they were trod upon. They exuded the overpowering smell of vegetation, but everyone called it *dibe bichaa'*. Sheep feces. Not a wonderful scent, but one that places me once again at the side of my maternal grandmother as she and mom decide which sheep we would butcher.

My grandfather sharpened the knives on the stone, though he might have considered butchering women's work when my mom participated. My Aunt Dorothy usually caught the sheep. Then my grandfather parked his truck near the corral gate. He hurried about in the background. He helped bind one front and one back leg with a rope as the sheep cried for dear life. I had no doubt then, or now, that the sheep knew of approaching doom. I saw the tension in the flock as they moved about in the corral, and once the chosen one was caught, the tension evaporated. The cutting of the neck and jugular was the noisiest part of the process because the animal fought for its life. Sometimes, even after the jugular was cut, the animal bleated and writhed. The blood shot upward and was caught into a bowl that my mom made into blood sausage.

Though this was one of my favorite dishes, I still felt compassion for the sheep. Once it came into the world, it followed its mother, getting to know her scent and her vocal sounds, growing and seeking the safety of the herd, seeing us, people, on foot or horseback, as it learned to graze and drink water. Then at the end of the day, it settled in the shelter of the corral. Life must have been predictably peaceful until the day a human, whom it has come to associate with safety, came baring a knife.

My mom told us that cattle learn to recognize a person's voice. She said she didn't know how much they understood, but she relayed stories of riding horses in blizzards or under the stars. A few times she had drifted off to sleep from fatigue, waking to discover that the horse walked its way home. By this time, I had had a lamb that I raised from the bottle. I

127

fed it and we took walks. I learned it could mimic my moves so well that if I skipped, it did, too. If I trotted, it did the same, keeping pace with me. It liked to run, and I believed it liked to race me. Once I shared my Butterfingers with the lamb. It ate it, probably out of polite obligation. I knew these animals were intelligent, warm, kind, and aware when death loomed. I always found an excuse to touch the coat and whisper, *Ahehee'* before the butchering began.

Once the animal was beheaded, another great meal was prepared. The juiciest meat are the cheeks. Tasty without any seasonings. Eyes and tongue were delicacies. I liked this best when the head was earthbaked. After the sheep's hide was removed and placed inside up, my mom and her mother hoisted the body up a cedar trunk that my one of my uncles erected for this stage of the butchering. Once hoisted, someone cut from the navel to mid-chest. Hands readily caught the intestines and other organs. In the cool early morning air, the organs steamed with life-heat, reminding me of the precious warmth and sacredness of life. I was assigned to help empty the contents of the stomach; I was given ropes of small intestines to hold. These were light jobs, but could easily become messy if the unprocessed contents spilled on shoes or worse, pants. The liver was sheathed in a white fatty sheet of tissue that I was often told to hold as it stiffened and stretched out. This fatty blanket was then cut into strips that the small intestines were coiled around after being cleaned. Another wonderful delicacy. Coiled intestines. *Ach'ii bikee deesdiz.* I can't think of any sheep parts I didn't like. It was all delicious, a meat eater's heaven. This was the only time that we had mutton. We grilled, stewed, roasted, and earth baked it. The fresh meat made it all the more delicious.

We rarely spent the night at my maternal grandparents' home. In the late afternoon, my mom wrapped the sheep legs in Blue Corn Flour material, to give to relatives. Sometimes she gave cooked meat, too. That night, as we had our sponge bath at the White House, my mom took our Saturday clothes and bagged them in a plastic bag that we took back to Phoenix for laundering. We put on our sleeping clothes. On Sunday morning, we wore clean clothes. Because we had to make the four-hour drive to Phoenix, we didn't stay long on those Sundays, but we all took time to breathe and step on Mother Earth, inhaling and ingesting, life. Before leaving, I made time to walk up to the top of a sand bar, where I stood and looked at our little valley. I wanted to memorize the land and vista, so I could replay the images until our next return. I also hid an unusually pretty pebble under a cedar bush or a rock to search for when we returned. Until then, the bush, the pebble, and I shared a secret.

We made our return in broad daylight; as the beige pickup was my dad's first vehicle, he had learned the hard way about maintenance and repair. A proud man, he didn't consult experienced vehicle owners about the how-to of repairs. I was given the role of tool retriever, handing him whatever he needed as he lay under the truck making repairs. He had trouble with tires for a while because he bought them used from local shops, but after having to fix many flats, he realized the wisdom of buying brand new tires. More than once we had to pull into an emergency lane to repair a flat, in the dark, while cars sped by on the I-17 heading towards the heart of Phoenix. Oddly, these repairs always happened at the end of a road trip, as if we were paying the dues of a long enriching family trip.

Before leaving the White House, I had the chore of sweeping and sometimes dish washing, but I was still a useless person when it came to the main housework. I carried out to the truck whatever we took back to our small Phoenix house. When we left, our beds were made, the water barrel lids were secured, everything was folded and stored away, the counter and table were cleaned and cleared, wood was stacked in the wood box, and the wood burning stove ash was removed. Sometimes a log was placed into the stove belly for our next return. My mom was the last person to walk through and lock the south door as we waited in the cab of the truck. She was also the keeper of the White House key.

However, once upon our late arrival at the White House, my mom searched in her handbag for that key, but even after emptying it into her lap, she couldn't find it. Then my dad went into a tirade. I listened to the disruption to the silence of the setting and looked at my mom's profile in the cab. What prompted my walk to the door, to turn the door handle, and see if the door was unlocked? I returned to interrupt the blistering onslaught, announcing with so much relief, *The door is open.*

Our getaways could have easily turned on a dime, but it harbored something greater than that as depicted by discovery, but I know we had trips, nothing short of miracles.

Generally however, our weekend getaways were about feasting, cleaning, and enjoying our weekend retreat, the role the White House had assumed since our move to Phoenix. If we had a three-day weekend, we headed to the White House. When we left for home again, we often had an ice chest with freshly butchered meat for our Phoenix meals. These were busy, wonderful trips. On the return drive, I studied the changing colors and textures of the landscapes in broad daylight. From the other side of Echo Cliffs, east of this rocky range, down to Gap, then to Flagstaff, down to Camp Verde, and then up and across to the plateau of Sunset Point where we stopped for a restroom break, then down to New River, and finally into the outer edge of the metropolis of Phoenix. We passed through the heart of Phoenix and drove on Central Avenue to turn right on Jones Avenue.

During the school year, Dean and I rarely missed school even if we returned late Sunday evening from our White House mini-vacation. In fact, I can't recall having ever missed school. I have very few memories of ever being sick in those early years. Perhaps that's why I remember my chicken pox experience so vividly. However, there was another time even before that, in El Monte, when I recall not feeling myself, so much so that my mom inquired what was wrong. She felt my forehead because I was out of sorts. Lying on the couch was not like me. Later she described my eyes moving about so dispiritedly that she worried. This too I recall like yesterday.

Shiyahz, what's wrong?

I only shifted slightly, feeling such burdensome fatigue that when I closed my eyes to blink, I didn't have the energy to open them again. Even trying to hold my mom's gaze from beneath my droopy lids was a battle that I was quickly losing. She did the best that any mother could do, holding me and murmuring sweetnesses.

She asked what I wanted to eat, perhaps wanting to gauge the seriousness of my illness. If I had no interest in my favorite food, I would certainly have been in a bad way. Sometimes caring and sympathetic skilled cooks, like my mom, know food can alter the course of a day. She knew sautéed sardines were one of my favorite dishes, but when she tried to tempt me with it, I barely had the energy to say, No. *Doo nisin dah.* Plainly she was worried. She got up to bring my drawing pad, along with my crayons and pencils in a small box. Perhaps she knew the importance of signs and symbols to me, so she asked, *How do you feel?*

I took a dark crayon and gripped it as firmly as I could, but when I pressed it against the pad of paper, my grasp slipped. I picked up the crayon slowly and tried again.

By now I knew most of my letters, and certain letters conveyed feelings as I drew them. For example, the little /a/ was full of anticipation, as though waiting for a companion to stand with. I could clearly see then that little /a/ liked company. It especially liked tall friends, like L, B, T, F, and H.

My favorite letters were B and E, as in my initials. It made perfect sense that the first letter of my name was a piece of the first letter of my last name. Both had strong backs and three prongs. The E was the almost of the B. It was an incomplete development of B, a symbol bursting with ideas, promise, and fullness. I also liked the O, C, and Q because they were circular. The same is true of the letter D and any letters with bellies or big heads or bubbles: P and G. I liked the up and down of M and N, similar to Z. It was like saying *yes-no-YES!* It was a mixture of feelings, but a playful symbol of zig zag. Some letters I didn't trust: L, K, I, and Y, even though I told myself Y looked like it was cheering me on. L looked like it was missing something, like it was lonely. It had a stray, unwanted aspect. Three Dog Night's "One is the Loneliest Number" spoke truth because when I drew the number one and a capital I, the number and letter created twin sadnesses. The capital and the small L were in a similar fix. However, when I looked at the capital H, it seemed hopeful because two letters had found one another and were holding hands.

I wasn't acquainted with all the attributes of my letters, but I knew they were to be my friends. I knew I would like them all, and when I saw a word I liked, I thought, *There are my friends M and S. Yes, this is a good word to know.* This monologue with letters and numbers made my introduction to them a positive experience, but in truth, I looked at the world itself as a place where wonder and discovery were to be had daily. I might see an ant treading a path by itself, scouting or returning to message others where there was food. Or I might see a child on a swing and wonder about its highest point, or exactly how the child leaned far forward and backward, or the way he folded his legs to propel himself so high, or what he might see from way up there. Or I might observe how the sun peeked through full summer leaves, how such small leaves could screen out great Father Sun. I made up riddles only I could answer because they were so peculiarly constructed: What's green and thin but can cover the sun? Leaves when I stand under the tree. What five items work like a team that push, hold, and grip? Toes, of course. What number looks like a rabbit or kangaroo leg? Two. What number is ready to spring? Two. What number is missing a back? Three. That's probably why my sketch pad had many of the same letters printed and repeated. I made up stories and dialogues for them as I copied their shapes onto my paper.

After my mom brought me my sketch pad, I drew random straight lines of varying lengths, then extended them so the edges met. I concentrated on my sickness picture, letting my physical turmoil lead me, drawing without preconceived images and motivated only by my mom's desire to understand my feelings. When I was done, I saw that I had drawn an outline shape like a capital L. I continued by drawing tiny specks within the large L, adding them slowly until I captured the congestion I felt bottled up in me, I showed my mom. She stared at the drawing for a while and finally nodded in understanding. *Dik'eh.*

Dik'eh means square or cube, but to me it also denotes trapezoid. The angles, whether acute, right, or obtuse, capture the feeling of disconnectedness: when nothing seems right. In Navajo, the rigidity of angles obstructs free flow. When that dome collapses into jaggedness. English words like sharp, acute, jagged, cracked, crooked, or skewed all suggest the visual meaning of *dik'eh*, but not the emotional quality of confusion, loss, grief, deflation, perhaps depression, certainly "out of sorts." If I had drawn a K, then my specks would have left some room for movement, but with an L, movement was limited. I felt stifled, listless, congested, and plainly out of sorts. The outline of the L captured my ailment.

My mom's wise nod confirmed that I had relayed my feelings to her. She knew I felt the sharp angles of pressure and immobility. She held me as I drifted off into healing sleep. While I regularly singed her last nerve with my endless energy, I alarmed her when I lacked this same energy. She stopped everything to hold me.

My brother and my near-perfect attendance at school was partly fueled by our mom's home-cooked meals. Certainly sunlight benefited us, along with bike riding and other outdoor activities. Youth was definitely on our side, and my parents were also sunrays of health. However, there were some exceptions to our healthy diet. My mom regularly walked by Pete's Fish and Chips, a stand alone eatery on the corner of Jones and Central Avenue. One day, her curiosity must have drawn her to the menu, because when she met us after school, she strode over to Pete's and ordered five burgers, called sliders, for less than a dollar. She carried the sack as Dean and I shot one another looks of delight and confusion. This was our mother! The great chef on Jones Avenue, the secret treasure of our small neighborhood. Needless to say, we quickened our pace, curious about this first-time purchase.

Once home, my mom placed three plates on the table and gave herself a cola. There was only one bottle, but we all expected to share it. Then she doled out two burgers for Dean and two for me. We were in new territory because we were eating at the table. That alone was different. My mom doubtlessly expected us to like our burgers but wasn't sure how she would like them and gave herself just one. She couldn't have expected much for fifteen cents. Dean and I didn't analyze the cost or the taste relative to the cost. We simply knew we were in fat city, glad to have another burger, albeit one from a bag and at our own table. Actually the bag and the table made it novel.

We unwrapped our sliders. I loved the sound of the paper as it crinkled apart, revealing my small burger. I smelled the yeast of the roll and when I lifted the top half, I saw the textured burger. When I took a bite, the meat seemed to decompose in my mouth. An old person like my *Nali Sani* could gum this with no trouble. I could taste the oils. My mom had taken out bottles of catsup and mustard and a jar of relish because she didn't know what the burgers would be like. Disappointments could be mitigated with any kind of condiment. However, these burgers were perfectly fine. I finished my first one in four bites. I gave myself ample chewing time, which slowed me considerably. Long before chewing 12-15 times was advised, I did it. After taking a bite, I chewed and chewed as I looked at my remaining burger, the paper, my plate, my mom as she took her suspicious bite, and my brother Dean. He didn't value my slow eating practice, and often asked if I wanted a certain item on my plate when his was cleaned. Sometimes I was generous and sometimes I wasn't.

I'm still eating didn't phase him. He gave me a look that was hard to resist and I caved in. I cut my remaining portion to satisfy him. I sometimes halved it again before I had a small last bite. When it came to the mini-burger, I wasn't giving up my second burger. I found the eating experience greater than the tasty burger itself. I enjoyed knowing that we were part of a larger society that enjoyed what we were having.

The sliders became an occasional treat that we didn't disclose to our dad, who came home hours later. It became our regular dinner when, on Fridays, our dad forgot about us and didn't come home at all. But this eating treat eventually ushered in other new food. While my mom kneaded and pan baked her naan-like bread daily, she made dad's lunch meals using store brought bread—the spongy kind. Our homemade meals were occasionally interspersed with what we called sliced yeasty bread. She used cold cuts and lettuce and topped it with mustard and a sprinkle of black pepper. She included an apple. When my meaning switched from white people bread to actual bleached white bread, I don't recall.

Another new experience was my mom letting me sleep over at my neighbor friend's house. My friend had asked twice before my mom gave the long-awaited nod. On a Friday night, I equipped myself with a sleeping bag, pillow, and change of clothes, presumed sleepover requirements. If I brought a courtesy snack, I have no recollection. I walked 25 steps from our front door to hers. We watched color TV, and I noticed my friend's family talked a lot more than my parents did. I liked the food: fried tacos, rice and beans, menudo, and lots of tortillas. The food was spicier than I was used to, and my friend's parents laughed when I opened my mouth to cool it. *Eat some rice*, I was told. Someone gently scolded another family member, *You gave her too much. She might get sick.* There was much laughter, but not at me. *Are you* OK? I was asked solicitously. I nodded and smiled, *Thank you.* Like Monica, my hosts called me Evelina.

In our neighborhood, children my age played together. We took turns on one another's bikes. We sometimes played kick the can, and we raced through back yards as we played. Occasionally we got a chastising, *Hey!* But for the most part, families were obliging. I felt I had a large family in our neighborhood. While I only visited a few in their homes, everyone shared a pleasant *Hello* or *Good morning*, or *Good-night* once the cicadas hummed and moths fluttered

Because of the Phoenix summer heat, games usually started after sundown. In the summer, my dad made me a tetherball stand. He welded a pole with a loop at the top to a base made of an old tire with a rim. He bought me a tetherball that I tied to the hoop by lowering the pole. To stabilize the base, we filled the rim with rocks. My dad may not have been able to say I love you, but building this was a sign of his love. When I stayed after school to play tetherball, I came home late, finding my mom in complete agitation. My dad mitigated this by welding together my favorite game, basing it on my description. Not a rocket-science construction, how did this contribute to my sense of self, the making of my essence? When I helped take my dad-made tetherball from the truck bed, I ran my hand along the steel pole, noting where my dad had smoothed it by sanding and buffing.

My friends and I spent many happy hours playing tetherball in the fading light. I loved the tension of the game, my stomach tightening in anticipation not only for my next move but from the fierce awareness that light was suddenly abandoning our game. Many games ceased midway because we could no longer see the ball. My brother Dean and I were usually the first to go in when my mom called us, but sometimes we were given a temporary reprieve by being allowed to play in the growing darkness.

All this combined to make me giddy with delight as I played tetherball. Some even accused me of poor sportsmanship because I couldn't contain my bursts of giggles as we played. As calm and composed as I was when I played board games, whenever I physically exerted myself, giggles erupted from a deep cavern of happiness. Nothing was worse than standing on the inside of the screen door listening to the play and laughter of others as the dark completely blanketed the neighborhood.

Somehow I caught lice in my summer play. My mom discovered them when she brushed my hair one morning. She first used the lice shampoo, but that didn't seem to cure it, so she upped the ante by applying kerosene to my scalp. I must have stunk enough that she wrapped a towel around my head and let me sit in the sun. Amazing that I didn't pass out or damage my eyes from the poison, although I must admit to being severely near-sighted today. I still have a great sense of smell but I no longer have that full head of hair that I had to battle in daily brushing. How much that was a result of the kerosene I'll never know, but I no longer had lice after the half hour in the sun.

Later my dad touched my head and said, *I'm glad you didn't light up today, Lebby,* as he sniffed my hair. He might have had his doubts about my mom's remedy, but since she handled all household matters, he didn't interfere with her decisions. In his own imperfect way, he was a noble dad, consistently employed for our family. In the evenings, we played a tic-tac-toe game I won at Brownies. My mom was very skilled at this. My dad and I laughed uncontrollably when we played.

That summer we moved from 313 West Jones Avenue to a nearby spacious, stand-alone rental with two bedrooms. It was on Third Avenue but farther from the street, so our address had a half added to it. I made sure to add this new detail when I labeled envelopes. I knew our mail box was on Third Avenue because I was the designated mail checker. Because I didn't know the mail carrier's delivery times, I checked the mailbox multiple times a day. I performed my new duty perhaps too zealously, an early hint of enjoying the rhythm of routine.

While we had yet to have a telephone, my dad's friends visited our new home. Those I remember best were Ophelia and Oscar, a handsome young Native couple. Oscar was tall and lanky with sideburns and glasses. He had an Elvis quality about him, probably because he played the guitar, had presence and was used to getting attention. When he chatted with Dean and me, he smiled and made eye contact with us. His wife Ophelia had long thick hair like the Breck girls we'd seen on TV shampoo commercials, but we had yet to see people of color in advertising roles on TV. Ophelia's hair would indisputably have qualified. Her hair was so heavy that when she lifted it with her hand, fanning her hair upward, I was reminded of the drapes in the Phoenix Orpheum Theatre. Glossy, heavy, very straight and so long that the ends hung to her thighs. Her hair had to be wound into a loose twist so she could sit down, and would naturally cascade down one she let it go. To me, there was Ophelia the person, and there was Ophelia's hair. While they were part of one another, clearly in my eyes they were separate entities. Like Peter Pan and his uncooperative shadow, Ophelia and her amazing hair.

Ophelia possessed great feminine grace, second only to my mom. She drank her Coke in sips and never monopolized attention, even when Oscar and my shameless Dad openly admired her. Even I liked her. When she laughed, she ducked her head slightly, and sometimes she laughed politely behind her hand. She was mesmerizing, a beauty queen in our midst. I liked her all the more when she giggled over games, teamed up with my mom against Oscar and my dad. The guys used brute force, but the women used strategy. Another lesson for me to remember. I also learned about my mom's competitive spirit. She earnestly felt she had the win way before the game started. Nothing would challenge that. Lesson two that day.

There must have been some secret drinking by Oscar and my dad, because they lingered outside, and with each return to the women and children, they became more boisterous. They reminded me of the boys in Resource class. While they didn't fly from the chairs or tables, their movements and voices became exaggerated. I followed them outside to see what altered them so suddenly, but all I got was, Hey, *go inside.*

My father was growing more confident about his drinking. Sometimes he disappeared for the weekend, and at times he brought home his beer cans. My parents were clearly divided on this. My dad most likely viewed the house as his castle and himself as the bread-winning man of the house, while my mom saw us, Dean and me, as her possessions. My dad dwelled in the here and now while my mom planned for our future. That summer, when my dad disappeared again, my mom quietly packed two suitcases of our belongings. She had us choose which toys we wanted to take with us, and when my dad arrived home, disoriented and with bloodshot eyes, tottering and ashamed, my mom presented her ultimatum. It was either his drinking or the family.

She said, *I escaped from a battle of drinkers. I thought you would help us, but you're repeating the same behavior as my family. You might take one or both of our children with you if I let you drink in front of them. But you won't take me. I will take them from you because you have forgotten yourself, your role, and us.* I have few memories of my mom being as forceful as she was at this moment. She was clear in her sense of responsibilities and her intent. Dean and I already knew about broken families. We had lived it at the White House. At times we had been reluctant to call our dad *nihizhe'e*, because he often didn't recognize us in public. Only when he was with us at home was his affection displayed. In public he was a different person. He used to dust us off, and that's what he began to do again. When he was paid, he now took his personal weekend vacations far away from us, making it clear that he had started his family too early and of his possible regrets.

My mom was right. It didn't make any sense to value school but to exhibit drunkenness in front of us. My dad begged her, and for a time he stopped drinking, but unfortunately it was like his North Star. He couldn't live without it. My mom believed that what he modeled would impact her children's future practice; she had seen this in her own family. She saw it in every one of her siblings. She was the only one who abstained from alcohol for all her life.

My mom never fully unpacked the suitcases, keeping them ready in the bottom of the closet. Whether because they served as a threat or because she didn't trust my dad's promises, the suitcases were always in a partial state of readiness. I felt the tension in the dark corners, in the closet, and behind the doors, just waiting to implode and change the life we knew.

The loss of my mom's dearest sister, whom my mom called Wilford *Bimaa*, to an alcohol-related accident while in a volatile marriage was a decisive experience for me though I never met this favorite sister of my mom's. She had promised to see my mom in the spring, after the birth of her youngest child, so they could weave together. My mom never got over the loss of her sister. Maybe that's why she wove so much: weaving took her to unseen settings where she communed with her sister again. Alcoholism haunted my mother's outlook on life. It was a palpable presence that resided in our home. That summer, when my mom showed me a Polaroid of a relative in his casket, I decided I would never drink. I could easily see myself in that place. While this relative was dressed in finery, he was dead. All dressed up with no place to go but into the ground. What sadness and disappointment for his family. Worse was that he probably knew and had heard many admonishments to stop drinking or make better decisions about his life. I felt that death, while still abstract, denied life's enjoyments, like recess, playing, bike riding, drawing, reading, watching TV, kickball, dodge ball, and swimming. Since all the deaths of relatives were alcohol-related, death and alcohol were synonymous, to me.

Children often believe that their parents are invincible. I did, until my dad came home early from work one day, surprising everyone. Normally, a half-hour before his return, my mom would set all of us into a flurry of cleaning. She ran the vacuum in the main household pathways, had us pick up odds and ends, had me move my paper and books off the table. It wasn't cleaning to the nth degree like Monday cleaning, but her tone became sharp during these 30 minutes. Perhaps because he granted all household duties to her, my mom prized her role. Dean and I were included in the term "household," so we were subject to her scrutiny and often her punishment. She transformed into an Old Testament mom until my dad parked the beige truck.

While our mom's punishment was sudden and stinging, a little on the wild side, Dad's was methodical. He kept count of our infractions. After the third, he belted us. He assumed a tired John Walton, Sr., style: *What did you do? Did you know you shouldn't have done that? Listen to your mother. All right, stand over here.* One or two belts later he added with a faint hue of guilt, *I didn't have a dad growing up, so I'm doing the best I can.* Still later, after he showered, we played checkers or he read and translated a news article aloud to us. When he was responsible dad, his routine was to come home and, while still in his uniform, ask my mom how we had been. If belting was necessary, that was the time. After he showered, he was relaxed and pleasant. He had the luxury of dividing his day—before work, work, after work—that my mom didn't have.

My mom was the last to sit down and the first to get up. However, she had many opportunities to witness my attempts at cunning. I didn't help her. I deliberately lowered the bar of my cooperation in household matters. I sloppily clocked and clacked dishes and cups together making what I thought were efficient dishwashing sounds, but when my mom inspected them, she saw through my show. Sometimes she put the other dishes back into the sink without a single word, or she dismissed me. She did this so randomly that I couldn't judge my advantages and thus determine her patterns. I could see my mom reigned over our household, her holy space, a space of safety for us and for her.

My parents were a study in double-bind theory in practice, perhaps a common theme in parenting and in life.

On most days, if I was outside when my dad returned from work, I could hear the rumble of his tail pipe long before I could see his truck. His carburetor was set too rich, he once told me. I wasn't sure exactly what that meant, but I could hear his truck before he entered the neighborhood. On this particular day though, my dad's regularly scheduled return time, as well as his invincibility, came to a sudden end when a beam fell on his foot at work. Though he wore steel-toe boots, his two toenails had popped up from the weight of the beam. He came home unusually early with his foot bandaged in clean white gauze. His toes had swelled, and very slowly he peeled off the tape and bandage. I sucked my teeth imagining his pain. My mom didn't have as much compassion as I had.

You can take the kids swimming, she said dryly.

My dad didn't expect this. I think he expected more fanfare.

The bleach and swimming will heal it. She said this from the kitchen where she was cooking. While my dad was taking time to digest her plan for him, Dean ran off to hunt for his swimming trunks. I stayed close to my dad to examine his foot. I wondered how he was going to get past the lifeguards at the public pool with his very ugly injured foot.

We ate traditional style, seated on the floor. I spread the tablecloth on the floor and placed the trivets for the pans. I laid down four plates, but my mom said to put Dad's on the table. We didn't use the table top to eat because this was where my mom cut out patterns and used her sewing machine. It was where Dean and I did homework or drew. When we had company, the adults might eat at the table, but Dean and I ate traditional style. Now injured, Dad was exiled to the table for dinner. This was a new family meal experience, Dad sitting at the table while we ate on the floor. Though this was a temporary arrangement, I could see how it reinforced his tendency to wander far from us.

The best outcome of this work-place injury was swimming daily for a week. My dad and brother wore swim trunks, but I didn't have a bathing suit. I could easily have gotten one from the thrift stores, as I had my Brownie uniform, but modesty prevented me. As much as I enjoyed wading in the water, I wore shorts that I called swim trunks and a T-shirt.

Now that he had the time, our dad decided he wanted to teach us to swim. His technique was very simple: He persuaded us to walk over to the deep end of the pool, where he quickly tossed us one after the other into the water. No warning. No mention of how to cup the palm to paddle. No demonstration of kicking. Just a quick toss. He stood at the edge of the pool to watch us.

Dean had it a little easier because his chubbiness gave him some buoyancy. I, on the other hand, had less, so I began to sink. I could see the sapphire blue shimmer above me on the pool wall as I sank. When my feet touched the bottom, I sprang upwards towards the edge. I broke the surface to hear my dad's instructions in fragments: *Come here, Shilebby!* The inability to rise and catch my breath was both new and overwhelming. I couldn't organize my thinking. I kept sinking, but fought my way to where my dad stood, motioning how to use my arms. Seeing others around me in the water assured me that this could be done. I just had to figure it out. I thrashed until I touched the pool edge, which had the firmness of earth and the comfort of safety. My eyes stung from the chlorine, but my ears took in the joyous clamor of shrieks of swimmers on a hot day in Phoenix. I coughed and heaved— what my dad found so entertaining and helpful still collided with my better judgement. Though I doubted my dad's method, it was a luxury to be in the water, to be with my brother, and to have this feeling of endless time until closing. My dad leaned down to announce, *You did it. You swam!* I turned to look at Dean. He spat out water like a fountain, bouncing as he dog paddled around me to show how easy it was to do this swimming thing. It remained a thing until I began to coordinate my arms and legs and learned to cup my hands. By closing time, Dean and I had graduated to the deep end of the pool, which had fewer people. My dad dropped a nickel into the water that we had to retrieve if we wanted to buy a Jolly Rancher from the canteen. Swimming for our treats. After swimming, we returned home.

I liked this new house, where I never saw gargoyles as I had in the shower stall of our previous home. This bathroom had a porcelain tub, and Dean and I didn't ever glimpse the shadow figure again.

When school began, my mother, brother, and I walked to Rio Vista Elementary for our second year of attendance. I was full of anticipation. Who would my new teacher be? My classmates? Where was my classroom? Where I would sit to learn? When was lunch? Recess? Gifts yet to be opened. We were welcomed by staff, all smiles, who directed us to my brother's classroom. Midway there, Dean shot off in the direction of a woman squatting to greet other students. I don't know if he yelled to alert her that he was barreling towards her, but she swung her arms wide and caught him, absorbing his momentum by turning to catch the last breath of his speed. What a happy reunion for Dean and his first-grade teacher! Her surprise and smiles said it all: she couldn't resist the charming presence of my brother. He was brown like most of his peers, with a dark head of hair, but he passed out his smiles like gifts. On the short side, he could easily squirrel into anyone's heart. I didn't know until then that my dear brother had to repeat the first grade. All those notes followed by beltings didn't make him listen or learn better, but at this moment his joy reflected the affection he and his teacher shared. I stood beside my mom, undoubtedly with my hair curled and wearing a new dress that she made the day before.

I had heard of *flunking*, and whether it was called *repeating* or *being held back*, the possibility of failure filled me with morbid fear, an end-of-the-world feeling that made me work like a demon in class. If someone learned something new, I made myself work just a little harder, not for the sake of I-want-to-be-first, but rather, I-want-to-be-part-of-that. I also knew that when I finished an assignment, I had time to draw, read, or whatever the teacher prompted us to enjoy. Sometimes it was clay, a Slinky, puzzles, checkers, or choosing a sticker. Stickers were great rewards. I decorated my notebook with them. Sometimes later when I was home, I carefully peeled the sticker off and attached it to my latest letter to my cousin Venne.

Knowing that Dean didn't advance to the next grade with his peers didn't sit well with me. I puzzled over this as we walked to my class. Mine was in the farthest southern exterior wing and tucked in a corner. When I saw Mrs. Monroe for the first time, she didn't stand out. She was tall and slender. She wore low heels and cat-eye glasses with tiny jewels in the corner that sparkled when they caught the sunlight. She wore lip color and her heavy brown hair was styled in a wave that she changed from one day to another. Sometimes on a Monday, it was straight bob with the ends curled, like mine was the year before when I was a second grader. Sometimes on Tuesday, it was up in a bouffant style. On the first day, she seemed unremarkable, although when she laughed later in the morning, she seemed to abandon it all, lifting her chin and letting loose, and I liked her more for it.

Standing beside by mom, I peeked inside the classroom, loving the colors I saw. My new teacher and my mom exchanged perfunctory first-day hellos. I walked into the room to find my seat. My name tag was placed on my desk next to the wall, and the desk faced Mrs. Monroe's desk. From where I sat, I could see the alphabet, in print and in cursive. I recalled my friend's sister telling me I would learn cursive, and she wrote her name to demonstrate, barely lifting her pencil. I asked her to write my name, so I could see how it was formed out of one connected line. I was struck by the artistry of this new way of writing. She told me I had to start in a specific place and that the loop of my Y had to go beneath the line. I pictured my poor Y in the water or soil as it pushed to transition to an N. Then the final curve of the lift in the N. It looked energetic and happy, like the last note of a song.

In the back of the classroom were two tables with folders, paper, pencils in cups, and more supplies, but what caught my attention was a painting of flowers on an easel. I couldn't resist its magnetic pull, so I got up and approached it. From my seat, the painting had appeared wet, but when I studied it from different angles, I noticed its texture. I could see how the brush strokes created layers on the surface to deepen the colors. This richness was almost too bright, brighter than what I knew from life, as if these images were from another world. Standing a few inches from the painting, what had appeared red from a distance actually revealed other colors. I saw splashes of black, brown, orange, and even yellow in the red.

It wasn't framed, but the artist had painted a frame onto the plank, depicting vines that reminded me of cursive. I couldn't take my eyes off it. While I studied the painting, the class had filled up with more students, and Mrs. Monroe touched my shoulder to say, *We're starting now, Evelyn,* as she walked by.

I wondered where she bought this painting with bursting, bright-colored flowers on a plank of wood. I had seen photographs or prints of paintings, but I had never seen an original up close. Mrs. Monroe's welcome and the care with which she decorated our classroom won me over. I was ready for whatever she was planning to do next.

Somewhere in this investigation of space and color, my mom disappeared. I never gave her much thought. This was the life of privilege to believe everything was for me and mine. I was that dreamy kid.

At the time, didn't know that my teacher was an artist who often sold her work. She asked that we draw ourselves as a means of introduction. Sometimes she brought in her paintings to display and to ask our opinions. We shared why we liked a certain painting more than another. We talked about the colors, how the red next to the green made it energetic or how the colors made us think of fall or winter or summer. Or how one flower next to another suggested company. One student said a big flower next to a small flower made him think of his mother and him. Mrs. Monroe recorded our comments, and then she arranged the paintings according to how much we liked them. She valued our opinions and listened, but she always went further: *Why do you suppose that is?* That single question made us dig deeper. Some said, *I don't know, but I like it.* When she heard that answer, she never responded in a way that caused the student to feel shy or to regret having spoken. She often rearranged the paintings to check whether our thinking had changed. Sometimes she said, *You are consistent.* Whatever that meant, she smiled when she said it.

The paintings I liked the most were the ones that she painted on wood rather than canvas. These paintings, so new to me, included nails of varying lengths, and on the flat surface of the nail was a continuation of what she painted on the wooden plank. Wherever I stood I saw a new perspective. Mrs. Monroe liked flowers, but she also painted cactus, roadrunners, coyotes, sunsets, and desert scapes. On Mondays my classmates and I became art critics as we responded to her work. Mrs. Monroe taught us to value our own opinions, a new kind of thinking for me. She used a similar method of guiding us to pay attention to our thinking to teach us math. I loved numbers because they were a portal to larger unseen possibilities. I saw numbers as the force of math. Sometimes I sat on the small of my butt to listen when Mrs. Monroe introduced a new concept in math. When she demonstrated a problem, she said, *Watch first,* as she worked the solution. The class became quiet. I liked this stage because it allowed me to think as I watched her write figures up and down and laterally—and then reveal the wonderful answer. In the silence, we heard chalk taps to emphasize certain steps and she smiled to herself as she worked the problems. I could almost feel the vibrations of her movements, the numbers as they fell into place, but most of all, her pleasure.

Because I was still learning English, this silent interval added a new, quiet moment to think as I observed. When I was learning a new concept, I required the utmost concentration, and having that silent interlude helped me grasp and solidify ideas. When Mrs. Monroe finished, she turned, tucking her hand with the chalk around her other arm as she smiled and asked, *What did you notice?*

We raised our hands and made observations about patterns, comparisons, and contrasts from previous math solutions. She nodded smiling. OK, *now for the same problem, but this time I'll tell you the steps as I'm doing them*, and she erased her first problem and began again. She demonstrated with verbal cues and clues added small alphabetical letters to remind us of her steps. She created a coding system that helped us recall the next step.

When we said, *Step B is next!* Mrs. Moore smiled.

It's fair to say that I loved this method. Sometimes she invited us to work in teams of two to solve problems she wrote on the board. The teams could talk and took turns passing the chalk when she said, *Switch the chalk, please.* This process helped me learned English, because we had to talk about our steps and the reasons we followed them. Our audience were our peers and our math master, Mrs. Monroe.

While we went over the math operations as a class, at no time did I ever hear our teacher say, *Evelyn, you got it wrong.* She often asked, *What should you have done?* If I didn't have a clue, she called on someone to help. This gave math solutions an exploratory air, as though we were in new territory, excavating a land in which the treasure or artifact was the solution itself.

After her demonstrations and our attempts to replicate what she had done, she distributed worksheets. She assigned odds or evens, and whichever we didn't do in class was homework. When we finished, we showed her our work. This meant walking up to Mrs. Monroe's desk where I stood beside her. As she checked my computations, I gazed at her hair, her nails, and her little nods, listening to soft murmurs that I called her thinking sounds. Before she said, *Looks good, but we'll go over it later,* she placed a small check in the left corner of the paper. That wonderful checkmark—a release to read or paint or play games or do puzzles. The last time I had water-colored on a big easel was in Park Elementary in El Monte, so this was a treat.

Two easels stood in the back of the classroom. Mrs. Monroe tore off butcher paper that we painted on. She showed me how to dampen parts of the paper to create a tie-dye effect. Sometimes she would said, *See if you can make the red brighter by mixing it on the paper.* Or we could be left to our own devices to paint what we wanted. Our paintings dried by afternoon, so we could take them home. Often, however, my painting took several days to complete. *Evelyn, I placed your masterpiece on the far easel.* Her call, *Clean up folks!* signaled us to put away our painting and supplies. I valued these small spaces of free time as rewards, privileges.

When everyone had completed the math assignment, we checked our work, even and odd problems. Again, we went to the board to copy a problem for all to see. With the help of peers, we had sufficient support to take our remaining math problems home for homework, because we could look at problems that we solved earlier as our guide.

The next morning, we checked our homework, following the same routine as before. Math taught me to listen, predict, study patterns, be neat, talk about my thinking, and model problem-solving in front of the class. I also loved the quiet when I worked on math. Mrs. Monroe played classical music or jazz on the radio as we worked. I can still hear the DJ's voice, breathy and upbeat for jazz and reverent for classical music. Math was a magical part of the day.

Math preceded another favorite time of day, and tension filled the air as we prepared for our well-deserved respite. Recess. We played red rover, freeze tag, dodge ball, and my absolute favorite, tetherball. Sometimes, returning to the classroom, we were so hot from the soaring Phoenix temperatures that Mrs. Monroe allowed us a cooling period with the lights turned off while the radio played. Sometimes we drifted into a nap. These were wonderful to wake from, like a mini-vacation after a long satisfying vacation.

I didn't have Mrs. Monroe for Reading. For that class I walked to another room, where I sat at someone else's desk. Curious, I peeked into the desk. Big mistake. The owner of this desk had a brand-new green pencil with a perfectly clean eraser. Impulsively I slipped the pencil into my boot, and resumed whatever class activity we were doing. I didn't give this a second thought, but later at lunch, several girls approached Monica and me playing tetherball. One girl said, *You took my green pencil from my desk.* It was true. I could feel the pencil still in my sweaty boot, but I was not going to admit I was a thief and appear in a bad light in front of dear Monica. It was hard to find a good tetherball partner, much less a friend. Instead, mercifully, Monica said, *Evelina does not steal. Someone else took your pencil*, as she slammed the ball mightily. That perfect move made the small crowd of girls flinch and move away together in their protective hive. I continued to play, but my heart wasn't in the game. The pencil in my boot had become a guilty itch, one that I couldn't unzip and scratch because that would reveal my sticky fingers and my lying ways.

I decided I had to remedy the problem I had created. I had to preserve Monica's good opinion of me, give the pencil back (as pretty as it was), and get rid of the guilty itch that had migrated to a place I couldn't scratch, and that I knew would only worsen in time. I was lucky that I wasn't good at stealing. This was the first time I had stolen something, and immediately the owner knew who I was and where to find me. I returned the pencil the next day by pushing it as far as I could reach into the desk. From then on, I forced myself not to look into that desk, or any others. I knew my resolve could weaken and I might take something. I would be discovered and called a lying thief. Third grade was perfect, and I didn't want to ruin it.

One day, when I returned to my seat after painting, I noticed my seat mate Fran was staring far off into space with an angry expression. We began to check our work, but this time, Mrs. Monroe said we had to exchange our work with a partner. I turned to give my work to Fran, and she slowly gave me hers. As instructed, I wrote my name in tiny letters at the bottom to show Mrs. Monroe who the student grader was. I wanted to sneak a glance at my own paper, but Fran avoided any eye contact. Meanwhile, Fran got most of her problems wrong. I wanted Fran to join me in painting, but if she continued to get problems wrong, she and I would never paint together.

The next morning, I brought my completed math problems to get checked off by Mrs. Monroe. She was seated at her desk, and as I stood beside her, I observed that the hair closest to her scalp was white, giving her a vague halo effect. Good Lord. I saw this as evidence that Mrs. Monroe was an even greater person than the one she impersonated daily. Whether it was biblical angels or Navajo gods, I believed angels and spirits were in our midst, so when I made the discovery of her halo, I didn't tell anyone, though my heart swelled almost to bursting with truth, unwilling to violate the trust I had been given through this revelation. I also believed this meant I could do some mighty works myself, after all I was part of a great pact, the secrecy of my new special knowledge of Mrs. Monroe's true self. I asked Mrs. Monroe if I could help Fran with her math, since I knew she would understand my intention and approve my request because she knew my heart. Her everyday disguise had slipped, and when

I glanced around the room, no one seemed to see what I had seen, confirming that I had received a special gift of knowledge. *Of course you can help, but you must help with the steps. Not the answers*, she said, putting special emphasis on *answers*.

Later when I sat beside Fran and helped her, I slowly repeated the steps we knew as the A, B, C, D, and E of various problems. I repeated them until Fran began to smile again, having worked a problem to its solution. Later, we painted together as I predicted we would.

One day I painted a picture of the rug my mom was currently weaving. It had a pattern of corns stalks and *yei bicheii* figures sheltered under a rainbow shield. It was one of her first designs. Later she would replace corn stalks with spotted serpents along with *yei bicheii* dancing, placed in alternating patterns, frightening her mother and my Aunt Sadie too much to even look at it. But this edgy design sold well. When Mrs. Monroe saw my painting, she stopped to examine it. *Tell me about your painting, Evelyn.* That's how an angel drove me home in a white car with a maroon interior that was big enough to hold a horse. When I saw her pull out a long skinny cigarette and, smiling, light up, I knew that one day I too would drive a big-assed white car and smoke long skinny cigarettes. I might never be an angel like Mrs. Monroe, but certainly I could have a white car and smoke, all the while loving math.

When Mrs. Monroe and I entered my front door, I called out to my mom that my teacher was here to visit. I explained to my mom in Navajo that my teacher wanted to see her loom. Only when I saw them together did I realize that I was witnessing two artists speaking to one another, and I was their translator. Ordinarily I translated for my mother from Navajo to English, but now I had a different task. I was translating from English to Navajo, to English, and back and forth. I'd advanced beyond my role of being my mom's translator, and the English speaker was no longer on TV but in our home. Before Mrs. Monroe left, she told my mom that I was a good student. She also said that I helped others in math (a tiny bit of stretching there, but she might have been hopeful), and that I loved painting. Most important of all, she bought one of my mom's rugs. The single experience made me want to work harder in my angel's class. My confidence bloomed.

Periodically our class visited the library. During these group visits, the librarian was kept busy checking in overdue books and offering us library instruction, including the Dewey Decimal System, book suggestions and reviews. Sometimes she even promoted a new title to us. With such generosity, it had never occurred to me to ask a librarian to help me find a book, and she wouldn't have had time to talk to me during our class visits. However, on one occasion I returned a library book earlier than usual, and our librarian, a very energetic woman with short grey hair, smiled and announced, *I believe you're ready for the Betsy books.* I followed her and on the very lowest shelf were several books with the title *Betsy. Let's have you start with* B is for Betsy, she said.

That's how I began the Betsy books. Perhaps it was the librarian's one-on-one attention that made the book so special. It wasn't long before I was ready to check out a new Betsy book.

That afternoon, walking home with my new library book tucked in the fold of my arm, I ran my fingertips along the edge of the outer pages. As my fingers fanned the pages, I was mindful of wanting to curl up with it to read, but I also felt Father Sun's lights play on my arms and face as if to remind me of the beauty of this moment. I was getting older and an adult I had barely spoken with noticed my growth. Not physical growth, but internal. These changes couldn't be seen in a mirror, but were observed through my actions. I had felt my angel-teacher Mrs. Monroe's confidence in me when I told her I had finished a book and wanted to go check out another and she wrote me a pass to do exactly that. As the sun warmed me with its love, I felt gratified by these educators' conviction that I could read this new fat book. The sun reminded me of what I had been entrusted with—a bond that I felt as a privilege. My mother didn't fully appreciate the fruits of sedentary reading, although I was increasingly directing my energy to such learning. Instead of riding my bike, I spent that time sitting on the porch lost in a book. If I were asked the name of a friend after I began this new series, I would have answered, *Betsy*.

In addition to my seat-mate Fran, I also knew Elizabeth, who, like me, rarely struggled with her school work. She had blondish hair, a little messy, which I found very pretty; she didn't have someone like my mother pulling at her hair every single morning. Elizabeth also had great fashion sense. She wore hats, floppy ones with flowers or headbands. She wore boots with heels that might have been a bit too big for her, but she managed gracefully. My mom still made me wear a dress to school every day, while I pined for pants like my peers wore. Some even wore shorts. I envied any girls who wore pants, especially blue jeans. I liked the ones that were stressed and frayed, long before they were in fashion.

In more important ways than her fashion sense, Elizabeth operated in a different planetary system than ours. She had a great knowledge base. She would answer Mrs. Monroe's questions, then take it a step farther by asking her own questions. Her inquiries fueled my curiosity. Somehow Elizabeth's inquisitiveness and articulateness elevated her to the level of Mrs. Monroe. She was this tiny adult in a child's body. Elizabeth genuinely knew a lot, and sometimes she challenged norms. At times she might even take things too far. One day she wore a dark wig. I was already familiar with how the Black girls' hair might be short one week and glamorously long and beaded the next, so Elizabeth suddenly having dark full hair was believable to me. Even so, I mistook her for a new girl when I saw her from afar, until she yelled, *Hi Evelyn!* I loved her ability to transform herself. She was fearless and unapologetically true to herself. When a boy pulled her wig off, Elizabeth picked it up and adjusted it, giving it a firm tug, then resumed our conversation as we kept walking. She always seemed to be one step ahead of our class. While we advanced from stone to stone, steadying ourselves to avoid falling, Elizabeth frontiered ahead. She had ideas, information, and a strong vocabulary. Even though I was a good reader—by my own self-assessed standards, of course—I didn't use the vocabulary from my library books, like Elizabeth did. Talking with her was like having a book talk to me.

Another striking personality was Melody. She had a splattering of freckles across her nose and cheeks, like ancient warpaint bestowed on the holy. She invited all of us to play a card game she called Concentration. After she expertly shuffled her cards, she placed them face down, and we tried to find matches. She gained the confidence of Ray, who I'd met in Mrs. Butler's class the year before. I liked Ray, and I noticed he liked Melody, especially her smile and giggle. If Melody's beanie dropped, he scrambled to pick it up and held it slightly out of her reach, raising it playfully. He never tossed it like some boys did. I felt a touch of jealousy that Ray and Melody seemed to have a bond. I saw Ray gaze at Melody for long stretches. My jealousy didn't fully bud because I liked Melody, too.

One day, Melody invited several of us to visit her home. She wanted to show us her animals. Dean and I had begged our dad for a dog, but he always said, *Nope. The landlord said no.* So the opportunity to see a pig, rabbits, hens, a rooster, dogs and a cat was a real treat. As far as I knew, Melody had a regular farm. A block or two before reaching her home, Melody suddenly turned to the three of us to say, *You guys, my dad's Black. I don't want anyone to laugh at him. If this is hard for you, you should go home.* As usual, I was slow to understand her meaning. *Was her father really funny looking? Or was the idea of having a Black dad funny? Is that really funny?* These questions now floated around my eagerness to see her animals.

When we reached Melody's house, it was a regular house, larger than ours, but with two sheds and fenced areas with shade shelters. She led us around to show us her animals, providing details about when and what she fed them. She also showed us how to find eggs in the hen house. While the rest of us went to the store for a carton of eggs, Melody found hers in her backyard. How envious I was. When her father came out, Melody introduced us. He seemed like a regular dad. He smiled and told us, *Don't go away,* as he returned to the house. Melody continued her tour, and before we were done, her father brought out glasses of Kool-Aid with lemon wedges. What a treat. Refreshments!

I admired many people that school year. People entered my orbit who modeled behavior I wanted to learn, but Melody always remained an important figure for me. She understood the complexity of race, what it meant to have a Black dad and how some might react to him. And yet she always hoped to find tolerance in people. Maybe it was her way of testing who was true. Melody had no interest in painting like I did, but I admired her ability to articulate a complicated topic in an upfront manner. She had already learned a great deal by third grade. On top of that, she was kind, tall, and wore flared blue jeans.

Discovering Melody's hidden farm animals made me aware of the different worlds each of us inhabited. And nothing made me realize how limited my contribution was to my own family than Mrs. Monroe asking what foods we helped prepare at home. My hand was one of the first to shoot up, but my reach slackened until I lowered it completely. Somehow opening a can of Campbell's Soup, pouring the contents into a sauce-pan, then turning on the faucet to fill the can and emptying the water into the sauce pan sounded too easy. Compared to my classmates' responses—*tacos, tortillas, burritos, enchiladas, empanadas, menudo, tostadas, lasagna, chicken casserole, fried chicken*—my Campbell's Soup announcement didn't deserve mention, although my dad praised my soup making. I sometimes made it for Dean and me when my folks went out on their dates, although my mom forbade me from using the stove. I think she was right to have her suspicions. Even when I stood over my soup, stirring and checking the flame underneath the pan, my heart was elsewhere. I prepared the soup to eat but found no joy in kitchen labor. So when my dad complimented my soup making, I believed I was indeed marvelous, though my pleasure didn't arouse a desire for greater accomplishment. Making Campbell's Soup was plenty. I already knew how to make a decent peanut butter and jam sandwich. Did I burn with envy at all the rich foods my classmates prepared? Hardly. I was already beginning to sense my mom had no confidence in my culinary skill because she rarely invited me into her kitchen. I watched her knead the dough, but I never offered to help her make her naan-like bread.

Two situations made me jealous that third grade year, however. One was Alfred, a big tall boy who stuck out his tongue to rub it against his two protruding front teeth as he worked his math problems. He had a habit of correcting people publicly. Unlike Elizabeth, who often whispered, *Actually, that's not true*, in a quiet, worried manner, Alfred scoffed by snorting and then laughing as he pointed out someone's error. He did this enough that I decided he was the most unlikeable person in our class, and probably the whole third grade. A big however was that, though I disliked him, I envied his letters.

When Mrs. Monroe introduced cursive, she distributed lined and dotted paper. The dotted line showed where to place the top of the lower-case letters. The solid lines regulated the height and where the lower loops dipped. We went through each letter and practiced in silence as Mrs. Monroe circulated around the room holding an eraser and pencil she used to correct a B that swelled out of proportion or shriveled, emaciated. More than once, she corrected my letters, some of which morphed into altogether odd-looking creatures. I was always relieved when I heard, *There you are. Keep practicing. You have it.* If she lingered too long nearby, it meant she saw something that wasn't right. If we did our letters correctly, she sent us to the board to model them. That was like getting a gold star for the day. Already Mrs. Monroe had asked Alfred to model his B, D, K, M, and Q, upper and lower. I admitted he had a gliding lightness to his letters that were consistently properly inflated and, I felt, ballooned with arrogant satisfaction that Alfred couldn't disguise. He never seemed to be in a rush, like I was. Teeth sucker that he was, he stirred my green envy. On top of that, I had one more reason not to like him. I had wholly expected to be adept at cursive since it was similar to art. My disappointment turned to jaggers.

The day I felt especially stretched to strain was when Mrs. Monroe praised Alfred's Ss. Upper and lower were perfect in Mrs. Monroe's assessment. Once again, Alfred was called to the board to model his letter S. I was not in the habit of dwelling on injustices. I felt there were plenty of things to think about and do that were much more entertaining than feeling resentment, but seeing Alfred getting another accolade from my angel-teacher was too much. I wanted cursive to end, so we could go the library, to music, anywhere other than watching Alfred demonstrate his perfect upper and lower Ss that resembled teardrops. I noticed he put a little point at the top of his lower S. I felt even worse once I acknowledged that Mrs. Monroe was right. Alfred had perfect cursive. Perhaps I felt all this positive attention on Alfred might motivate him to change, but it didn't. He still had a mean streak. All those compliments were wasted on him. Yes, I was jealous and rather hateful about it. I certainly didn't model Elizabeth's or Melody's patience and generosity. I was far too deep in a cesspool of jealousy to see or think straight.

Later when we compared notes, Elizabeth accepted that her letters were far from the standard. She tucked her paper away after she looked at it and said, *I obviously need more practice*. On the other hand, Melody laughed at her cursive. She pointed out where she struggled with letters. Not cheered by their generous self-assessment, I chastised myself over a subject that I had looked forward to since the previous summer.

My second encounter with jealousy occurred when we got a new addition to our class. She was slight with loose clothes and dark hair, but she had light blue eyes. I don't recall her name, but it could have been Helen or Hazel. When she finished her math, she and I painted in the back of the room. She painted a single figure but in a range of colors and settings: Horses with thick manes and tails that were alive. Sometimes she painted pintos grazing or a stallion poised on a mound of grassland in a noble pose. Her horses were real. I watched her scrutinize her painting as she barely breathed. She saw something I couldn't see. Mrs. Monroe went overboard admiring the new girl's painting. In fact, our teacher pulled out a paint set with several sheets of paper for this horse-crazy girl with blue eyes to take home at the end of the day. Sometimes when I was home, I looked for horses in *National Geographic* to copy into my sketchpad, but the truth was I wasn't particularly fond of horses. Sure, I rode them. I liked how they smelled and their masses of muscles and how powerful they were, but I didn't care to draw them. When I did, I could sense it was to please my teacher, and that didn't feel quite right. I think Mrs. Monroe loved the passion the new girl had for horses and how she was able to capture that in her paintings. I didn't envy her paintings, but I was jealous that my angel-teacher admired someone else's work. That was it.

By contrast, I didn't feel any jealousy about my brother Dean when my mom showered him with attention. He was my little brother. He should be loved. After all, I loved him, too. Maybe I just needed to get to know the new girl. However, she was very shy. She ate quietly and lingered off to the side, away from the third-grade static. We were an electric storm, but she was a low hum, like the faint classical music that sometimes played in the background. I only saw her on the playground once. I was returning with Monica from our tetherball game, just before the final bell ended our lunch recess, when I saw the new girl standing by herself near a teacher. Her posture suggested a lone colt, lost from its mother, gazing towards a distant horizon.

Once a week, music took me to a new and wondrous plane. We sat in assigned sections in the music room, overseen by a teacher who needed a haircut. His bangs, which he flipped back constantly, were forever falling into his face. He never surrendered to irritation, not from his bangs nor from the squeaking sounds we made on our recorders. He had this very cool chalk holder that gripped five pieces of chalk, which he used to draw the scales for musical notes. He then drew the clef. I loved how the clef curved and seemed to announce, *And now*, before the notes danced in. On day one, he distributed recorders as we entered the room. Perhaps he wanted to make the most of the short time we had, or he loved music, or he loved children trying to make music on recorders. He never wasted any time getting us started. Because we sat alphabetically, I usually sat near the top tier. I sometimes watched the antics of the boys below, but we launched into whatever piece we were playing despite them. How our teacher could hear our notes, well, that was a study in listening skills. With every class period, the less engaged became more engaged. Music class was precious to me. Sometimes a mysterious man known as The Principal popped in unexpectedly, and at times he would motion a clown out of the room. In those days, corporal punishment was still practiced. I had heard that teachers whacked the sense in or out of students. I never wanted anyone to snap my behind ever again like Big Hair Bun had done. But there would certainly be no need to because this music class took us to new heights. We learned about notes, and now when I listened to the radio, I imagined musicians following musical notes on a staff as they played. What a marvelous secret world music had. What's more, it had a mathematical quality. Where each note was placed on the staff translated to a sound, and that sound could be attained, with lots of practice of course, by where I placed my fingertips on my recorder. In class, Long-Haired Teacher Man would demonstrate a small section of a larger body of music. He chunked the pieces. When we learned a small section, we then started from the top and played what we had memorized up to the new section. While he was facing us, he showed us the finger choreography, but he also turned his back to us as he held up his recorder to model as he walked from right to left so we all were able to see his finger placement. He moved to different places in the room to model for our viewing. Pretty amazing. We didn't sound wholly unified, but we played. This was perfect for my Navajo upbringing. I heard my folks and elders say *iists'aa* for listen, or the intense version, *ha'ahsiid*, observe with all your senses. I always imagined a hawk or an eagle flying high above the earth searching for shadows or detecting the minutest of movements to catch a critter.

As in Mrs. Monroe's class, I learned to sit quietly and observe with all my being although sometimes I glanced at Elizabeth or Melody for confirmation. Often a student near me modeled the finger-tip positions for others. In some intuitive way, we knew we were in the presence of greatness with Long-Haired Teacher Man. Before class was over, we got up row by row, placing our sheet music in one box and recorders in another, then walked in orderly fashion back to my angel-teacher, who was ready to welcome us. I was so proud that I hadn't uttered a note of her secret identity to anyone. By then her whitish halo had largely disappeared, but sometimes when she checked my math, I saw it peek out like a ray of light.

Long-Haired Teacher Man sometimes gave us half a sheet of paper and distributed pencils, asking us to write the notes he played, after which he checked our general cluelessness. He also had us demonstrate two or three notes, then inquired which notes So-and-So had played. The answers were always easy, but it was nice to have the right answer every time. Then he instructed us, *Write the notes down.* The association of sound, identification, and recording of the notes, including flats and sharps, fully engaged our senses. Soon when we learned a new section, I could identify each note by letter, and whether it was a full, half, or quarter note. I had no musical aspirations, but learning music this way involved a new way of thinking, and I looked forward to music. I suspect many of us did.

As spring sprung, suddenly things changed at home. My dad got a new job. He still welded, but a new job meant changes. My parents were ready to move elsewhere. My folks were young, so packing up our place and putting our boxes of belongings into the back of the pickup was easy. I had one day to say goodbye to my friends and Mrs. Monroe. I was going to attend a new school, my fifth new school, my second one in Phoenix, my third day school. Our unannounced move was very close to spring break of the school year.

What prompted such a sudden move? Perhaps that we knew a Navajo family with four children who were more and more often dropped off at our home without notice. The children were terrified of water, they could not eat sitting still, and they cried endlessly. When the children's parents wanted a night out or a weekend getaway, they sent their children our way or they locked them out of the apartment. The "We are *Dine* so you-are-to-help-us" is a great philosophy for maintaining unity among indigenous tribesmen, but not this time. I worried that my parents would one day drop off Dean and me at this family's apartment as reciprocation for our free-child care. My dad might have considered that because the children's mother was very pretty, with long wild hair, a bleary-eyed look, and very full red lips. My mom didn't share his appreciation of this wild mother-woman, and I wasn't happy that our home had become a noisy compartment. Or maybe we moved because my dad was the wild one and kept running off to be cared for by other wild women. My mom's permanently-packed suitcase had lost the power of its threat because my dad was once again overly-confident. Or maybe my mom's health declined as a result of husband-created stress, and this move brought her closer to the Phoenix Indian Medical Center, where she was a regular patient. Or maybe my dad wanted to be closer to his haunt, the Esquire Lounge, a Native bar on 7th Street. When the children were dropped off with us, the feeling in the house changed, and I went outside to read, but my mom needed me to help her with the crying young ones. I had no idea what to do. I told myself I would never have children of my own. Never. The children's cries cemented my decision.

I'm sure my mom had similar sentiments, though more like, *I can't keep doing this. I want my house back.* My dad's solution was easy, *Let's move.* The Let's-not-tell-them was never uttered.

Because of the abrupt nature of our move, leaving was sad for me. In the thick of painting, playing tetherball, learning the recorder, reading books, and flourishing under the wing of my angel-teacher Mrs. Monroe, I was yanked fiercely away. I never played the recorder again.

We moved to another one-bedroom apartment house. This house still stands and has become a quaint efficiency on Roosevelt Street in a budding historic district of downtown

Phoenix. At the time, of course, it was very affordable. We lived on a busy block of Roosevelt, and my mom had to turn up her radio to offset the noise of the street traffic. The front door faced north, so whenever I emerged from the house, I blew a breath to our lonely White House four hours away to the north. Our back door faced south, and when I came out, I could see part of South Mountain. The house was fenced, and the back had a wall of oleanders, so we had a secluded back space, along with a carport. The landlord had laid out a large green mat over the concrete. Once my dad strung a clothes line and set up my mom's washing machine, we called this new place home.

At the earliest opportunity, my mom enrolled us in our new school. We walked down Roosevelt for five blocks and turned right on Thirteenth Street to find Garfield Elementary School. It was a brick building with so many trees on the playground that later we used them as home base when we played freeze tag. My mom must have had faith in this school or in us, as she dropped us off and left. Kaibeto Boarding School was far away and had likely faded from her memory, but not from mine. I didn't forget Mr. Bird, Big Hair Bun, and Mr. Carrot. I still haven't.

My new teacher, Mrs. Querry, was tall and slim, but quite weathered. She could easily have retired years earlier, so challenged were her sight and hearing. She had a faint smile and a hollow, whispery voice. She smiled at me and announced, *Class, this is Evelyn. Please welcome her.* I barely merited a glance or two. Mrs. Querry said, *They're busy, as you can see.* I didn't see that, but we all perceive things differently.

Two names still echo clearly from this class: Manny and Jessie. Manny was a tiny boy with a big laugh that made up for his size, and he always found reasons to laugh. This included laughing to announce he wanted to say something. He had trained the boys around him so well that when he broke out in a laugh, they all turned to hear what he had to say. I soon learned that when Manny smiled at his male comrades, he was simultaneously engaged with his shoe. I realized that he would stick out this foot strategically, having hidden a small mirror underneath the laces.

When Mrs. Querry doddered by, Manny stuck out his foot to peek under her three-quarter length dress. Mrs. Querry had a fondness for long brown calico dresses. Old fashioned cuts along with heavy, opaque hosiery and granny shoes similar to those worn by the neighbor-witch who pedals into the tornado in *The Wizard of Oz*. Those were Mrs. Querry shoes. She was not a witch, not even close, but her third grade class was out of her hands, quite beyond her. Somehow the class settled enough to allow her to deliver lessons, but it was an every-man-for-himself learning approach. I received a math book and a primer, and other texts were distributed if we happened to get to them. Usually not. I brought my notebook with filler paper and a pencil the first day. I took them home daily because I didn't trust that I would find them the next day. I saw students rifling through Mrs. Querry's desk when she turned her back, but she moved so slowly they were never caught. Should she happen to turn, the boys ducked and crawled on all fours to get back to their desks, gripping whatever they had pilfered. If Mrs. Querry discovered a student on his hands and knees, he would rise and announce, *Here it is! I found my pencil, Mrs. Querry!* It pleased her to see how rapidly the student returned to his seat. I doubt she heard the laughter. I had joined a larger version of a Resource Room.

Jessie is the other student I recall. He too was slim, but he was taller than Manny, and was occasionally attentive in class. When, in arithmetic, Mrs. Querry introduced greater and less-than symbols, I didn't get it. Jessie swiveled in his seat and wrote to me upside down, *Less than two. The point always goes to the lesser number. The two is the bigger number.* Then he said, *Greater than two.* Followed by, *See how the arrow points to two? Now that's the lesser number.* Thanks to Jessie, I understood this simplification of the narrowing point to mean lesser, which had an echo in a Navajo concept of *dik'eh*, and I used the opening of the symbol as a chimney opening in a Hogan to show the vastness of the sky. I appreciated Jessie's teacher support practices.

I followed the crowd on the first day, and tried to find students who were academic survivalists, since I knew I would need their help. They were there, but were hidden behind the chaos. Mrs. Querry was kind, too. She smiled and welcomed everyone every morning, and she let yesterday be yesterday. Today was a new day. There was Manny adjusting his little mirror, while someone else was filing his nails, then pretending to use the file as a knife. I saw an actual pocket knife or two on my very first day, as well as students playing cards. But they weren't playing Concentration as Melody had. No.

On the first day, I was called a *Mojave* by a pretty girl with golden highlights in her hair. She said, *Mojave*, looking directly as me. I think it was a challenge to gauge what I was made up of. I stared at her until she looked away. She got no other reaction, so she turned to engage with more interesting friends. I had been called *Cheena Girl* a few times, probably because of my narrow eyes, but I let that fall by the wayside too.

At the end of the day, when my mom walked us home, I announced my refusal to wear dresses to school anymore. I don't recall if I told her about Little Mirror Manny, but I was adamant. Absolutely no more dresses. For all I knew, Little Mirror Manny might already have viewed my panties the first day of school, or as I was busy staring down Fria when she called me *Mojave*.

Nothing stands out for the remainder of third grade under the supervision of kind but ancient Mrs. Querry. We did hold an end-of-year party. We each called out what we would bring to the party. Mrs. Querry wrote our names and food items on the board. On party day, very few followed through with their pledges. I was likely one of them. While my mom made bread daily for our dinners, she didn't bake any sweets. We did not know of brownies, cookies, or fun pastries. These were not part of our meals. In fact, I didn't have these baked goods until I was two years older when I sampled fun food other people made. Occasionally I'd try to get my mom to buy a boxed cake mix that I swore I would make and clean up afterwards, but she walked away without any acknowledgement.

The closest market in our new neighborhood was on Pierce and Ninth Street, an Asian-owned market across from a drug store with an appetizing array of penny candy on the counter. Next to the drugstore was a laundry. All three businesses were owned by the same family. The family parked their sedans in a fenced and padlocked space. Like the rest of us who spoke Navajo or Spanish along with English, they spoke Chinese among themselves. They might have experienced some race or class tension because they did not greet customers and sometimes followed a shopper around the store, which caused those tensions to rise. It was best to hurry in, buy whatever items would tide us over until we could do a major grocery store visit, and leave. The store windows were barred, so the shops had a prison-like air.

When the day of the party arrived, a good number of students didn't show up. Manny was there, smiling, holding his bag of Doritos. When Mrs. Querry called for the party items, Manny unrolled his already-opened bag of Doritos and took a handful of chips before walking to the table where Mrs. Querry stood, ever so patiently and smiling benevolently.

CHAPTER 5

Fourth Grade: Train and Boxcars Journey

Perhaps it was to muffle the noise of traffic on Roosevelt Street, or perhaps she had always wanted one, but my mom bought a turn-table stereo. In the one-room house my dad had built, we'd had a manual record player, and I'd listened to songs as I steadily turned the crank. The selections on the sturdy vinyls were limited to hymns and lectures in English. The cadence of the lecturer was sing-song, and the voice had a booming, artificial quality. Despite that, I listened intently, straining my ears at the words and their meaning. Surely they must be important words if they were on a record.

    My mom's new record player had a fine tip needle that she would gingerly place on the groove at the record's outer edge. After she sold her most recently completed rug, she brought home a cellophane-wrapped album. I watched her use her fingernail to puncture the cellophane and slide out the white sleeve, then place the record on the record player. Those few seconds after the needle touched the vinyl but before the music began filled me with suspense, no matter how many times I heard the record. It reminded me of the instant before the curtains parted and *Pinocchio* began. Or listening as my dad turned the key in the ignition after he had done car repairs—just that fraction of a second before the engine fired up and rumbled back to life. These were slivers of time when I held my breath in expectation.

I knew that if mom had to choose between the TV, which all of us watched except her, and the record player, she would choose the latter. I might have sided with her at times; I don't recall being overly enamored with TV-land. I liked *The Undersea World of Jacques Cousteau*, *Wild Kingdom*, the *Wonderful World of Disney*, and one cartoon, *The Adventures of Jonny Quest*. *The Wallace and Ladmo Show* was falling out of favor with me because it was so predictable. I had memorized the skits, the cartoons, and the gifting of Ladmo Bags. Now the only fun was predicting the next skit. My interests were branching out. I loved listening to the radio, but I was starting to notice what music *I* liked, as opposed to my parents' preferences.

My mom's album collection started with Johnny Cash. Then came others: Dolly Parton, Charley Pride, Loretta Lynn, Buck Owens, Cole Porter. My mom's favorite was Elvis Presley, while my top two were Dolly Parton and Charley Pride. I loved Dolly Parton's pageant of stories, one about a colorful coat, another about a red-haired temptress, still others about mean dogs, faithfulness, and unfaithfulness. I felt a connection with Dolly's childhood, although my family was tiny next to the twelve children in hers. But she knew what it was like to live close to nature, to get by on bare-bones basics, and to yearn for the out-of-reach. As for Charlie

Pride, thanks to Melody, I was aware of his special place in country-western music, and I prized this along with his voice and songs. When I sometimes watched the sitcom *Hee-Haw*, I saw an all-white cast. Why had they never invited Charley Pride on as a guest? My favorite Charley Pride songs were "Kiss an Angel Good Morning," "Is Anyone Going to San Antone?," and—my all-time favorite—"Kaw-Liga." Dolly's "I Will Always Love You" ached with heartbreak, but "Kaw-Liga's" fate as a wooden statue captured the essence of true yearning and loss. Like Pinocchio, when he was a puppet, Kaw-Liga would only know isolation, loneliness, and terrible, unfulfilled desire. I played these songs over and over when I was alone.

In time, my mom's interest in other bands grew, and I learned about the Navajo Sundowners, a Navajo band that sang cover songs. The depiction of the band opened up a newly depicted Native world to me. Thanks to Ophelia and Oscar, I had met the Native version of Elvis and Priscilla Presley, but there was something unique about seeing Native musicians posed on a glossy album cover. For a long time, I'd been aware of nods to my heritage in the Phoenix Indian Medical Center, the Heard Museum, Canyon Records, and the Phoenix Indian School on Indian School Road, but while these institutions tapped into bits of my identity, they missed much more. One particular album featured a Navajo musician posed on a glossy cover. He wears turquoise and has shoulder-length hair. For someone who hadn't encountered mainstream depictions of Natives beyond those on TV

181

westerns, this Navajo musician let me see myself as others might see me. I immediately spotted the high cheek bones, straight hair, and ramrod straight posture. I was vaguely aware that some of us might be seen as having short necks, a result of early cradleboard constraints. I was seized by moments of recognition—*That's me!* It was a tad unsettling but also an important acknowledgement. Ah, *my tribesmen!* Still, I wasn't quite ready to join them.

My heritage was woven into the fabric of home; Navajo was our household language. I never felt shame, and I never believed that English was in any way superior to Navajo. I could not imagine speaking English in front of my mother outside of translating for her. She was a presence, as my Navajo language was a presence. When Dean and I walked to school, we quite naturally switched to Navajo at times. If we were in a group, we never prefaced our entry into Navajo with *Excuse me*, but simply broke into our language to stress a point or share a reminder. Was I aware of the power I felt in my mother tongue? Knowing that I was *Dine*, The People, undoubtedly nurtured my sense of identity, but Spanish was also spoken in my presence, so I also sensed Navajo as part of a multi-language community. I was definitely attuned to what communities shared more than what separated us. I didn't distinguish between Spanish speakers from Mexico, Honduras, or Panama, and when I heard White Mountain Apache, I honed in on similarities with Navajo, not differences.

I don't recall any teacher asking me about my culture. The only teachers who expressed an interest were Mr. Bird with his fiancée's mocha-skinned rag doll gift and Mrs. Monroe, who had purchased my mom's rug. I never felt that I needed any affirmation or that I wrestled with my Navajo identity. I liked my name, and I generally liked myself, and I never shied from forming friendships or the chance to talk with anyone if I was curious enough. My curiosity had a powerful pull, and it lent me a dreamy quality. Sometimes when I finished a book, I was sad to let it go and return it to the library. When narrative suspense or character conflict rose to intolerable heights, I would peek a few pages ahead to ease the knots in my stomach. This may have been intensified by my belief that the world revolved around me. I treated discoveries as events that were merely waiting for me to take notice. The thrill of fear or rising tension in a story were not mere distractions for me, but all-enveloping life experiences into which I plunged. This might occur as I walked to school, ate dinner, rode in the pickup with my family, did my chores, or whenever I found myself alone.

Complementing my escape into fiction was my habit of sweeping unsightliness into dark corners. In that sense, I was not all that different from my relatives. I doubt my Aunt Sadie and *Nali* had forgotten about my rape, but they never brought it up. My mom knew but kept her knowledge well-hidden from the light of day. No one denied that it had happened. It was still there, just never spoken of, even by me. Not the rape nor the abuses at Kaibeto Boarding School.

Visits to my *Nali* and Aunt Sadie had resumed after a period of silence, and I was once again free to roam outdoors with my cousins. One day during the summer before I entered fourth grade, as we stood outside my *Nali's* hogan deciding what to do, someone spotted a white form, a human shape gliding and bobbing along in the distance. All of us—my cousins Venne, Dan, and Marilyn, my brother Dean, and I—saw it clearly; it briefly melted away in direct sunlight, then reappeared on its journey once it moved behind a juniper. We watched it float towards the southwest from Teen's *Ma Sani's* home, observing it in utter silence, afraid to break the spell. I interrupted the hush to propose we follow it, but when I moved, my sister-cousin Venne gripped my shoulders tightly, with her usual *Are you stupid?* roughness. I didn't see the white figure as threatening. It was traveling, obviously governed by its own motivation, and I was curious. It spoke of nothing of the fears some harbor about phenomena. Seeing it move with direction, I saw some of our fears might have been unfounded. If I were able to chase it, would it evade me like a rainbow touching down just out of reach? If we had seen it at night, I might not have been as bold, but in broad daylight, if Venne hadn't held me so tightly, I would have run after it.

When the apparition disappeared, we returned to the here and now, and one of us told my *Nali*, who promptly hurried us indoors. *Leave it alone. Stay inside. Don't talk about it.* Later, in contrast, my mom listened quietly and cuddled us playfully, saying, *Yei!*, meaning *Boo!* or *Watch out!* Her reaction was not riddled with nameless fears. Maybe having witnessed her own mother practice hand trembling, I understood she trusted a greater presence. At any rate, she wasn't afraid.

Our mother was someone to be reckoned with. She revered her tools. She placed her weaving tools in a denim tool bag she had sewn. She also had a sewing toolbox with a thimble, an array of needles, rainbow spools of thread, a measuring tape, seam ripper, and bobbins. She was a skilled seamstress, though when I once asked her to make clothes for my dolls, she displayed a deaf ear. During a summer week at the White House, I asked my mom again, this time within hearing distance of my cousin-brother Dan. Approaching me later, Dan pulled out a piece of satin fabric from underneath his shirt. He spread out the material and asked me, *What shall we make of this?* The fabric had a magnificent magnetic quality. Its sheen, softness, and vibrance, along with Dan's generosity, left me speechless. I touched the fabric and touched it again, imagining how pleased my doll would be to wear such finery.

In another life, Dan might have been a fashion designer or a tailor. He made my doll a dress, along with matching summer wear consisting of a short-sleeved shirt and shorts. He sewed mostly by hand and reinforced his work with our grandmother's black Singer treadle sewing machine. In exchange for these clothing treasures, I was never to tell anyone. He threatened to make me cry if I reported his talent at design or sewing. He was only four months my senior but more adroit than I would ever be. He was also more generous than I was, despite pilfering fabric from his grandmother and mother. We never played dolls together, but he stayed nearby to observe and occasionally adjust clothing. If I left my doll behind somewhere, he retrieved it for me. Dean was my younger brother, but Dan was the older brother I never had.

My cousin-brother Dan was often our first visitor on Saturday mornings at the White House. Courteous to a fault, he always brought firewood when he visited in the early morning. He helped me with chores and helped my mother even more. It was at this time that I noticed the effect my mom had on others. Maybe it was her youthful promise or energy, but people wanted to assist her or simply be near her. To her credit, she didn't use this magic of hers indiscriminately, but to learn from others in her presence. A talented weaver, she created unique designs, and her talents sparked her curiosity about other handicrafts like Apache wedding baskets, Navajo baskets, kachina dolls, and silversmithing. She would, over time, produce these and more. If we went into a thrift store, she often told me to look for *National Geographic* magazines that displayed art on their pages. In my search, I discovered *Arizona Highways*, a local publication that included Native arts and crafts, and the stack on our coffee table grew.

The magazine issues that my mom especially liked were kept near her loom. While she was an industrious weaver, she would sometimes rev busily, then slow down to listen to our comings and goings, then come to a complete stop. When that happened, watch out. She was quick and merciless when angry, practicing the "mete out the punishment first and ask questions later" style of justice. More often though, she modeled the life of an artist-in-residence in our home. Some of the most endearing moments I recall were those when she sat quietly, lost in reverie as she studied the photographs of art in magazines. Sometimes she took a magazine into the kitchen and propped it up in her line of view, keeping the pages open with wooden clothesline pins as she prepared a meal.

That year my mother modeled for me the importance of quiet learning—manipulating an object until it fell into the place for which it was intended. When my mom, using black wool, completed the last outline or rainbow in her rug, she seemed to hear an inner art instructor advising her that her rug story was nearly finished. I want to believe that it was her long-deceased sister Wilfred *Bima* who then thanked her for the visit and departed until a new rug was begun. I still believe it was this sister who inspired the serene smile that appeared on my mom's face when the rug was completed, but I spied them when she thumbed through the magazine. What inner dialogue did she have from beyond our living room walls and what we called space?

My mother's weaving odyssey resembled my own as I drew pictures, but I didn't have my mother's patience to persevere to the end. My sketchpad featured unfinished drawings. I got stuck on the intricacies of hands and feet, two endings that eluded me. Over time I spent many hours drawing my hands and feet to see how creases became folds, or a fingernail disappeared behind a knuckle.

My cousin Dan must have felt a great desire to assist my mom, his aunt, because she was exacting. When she had a willing assistant like Dan, she simply called out what she needed. It was endless toil as far as I was concerned, but Dan complied cheerfully. Maybe it was gratifying to be in her presence, a nice change for him, the way I felt when I visited a friend's house and helped wash dishes or clean up before my friend was permitted to play. Dan and Venne were the children my mom might have wished she had. She praised them, and for children not used to receiving kind words from a maternal figure, I'm sure my mom was like a warm embrace. I liked having Venne and Dan around because that gave my mother less time to observe me and my doings, which in her eyes never seemed to land in quite the right light. All that aside, my brother Dean and I just loved our cousins' company.

Dan also helped my dad with wood chopping and hauling. If we went to see my *Ma Sani*, Dan sometimes stayed back with my dad to do home repairs. I don't know how my dad was viewed by others when we visited home from Phoenix, but I think people readily accepted this more responsible father among them. When I say *them*, I mean my paternal grandmother—my *Nali*—and my dad's older sister Sadie. They were the matriarchs and leaders in our home area, and my dad was reluctantly propelled back into their orbit. Obviously, he loved them, but I'm sure it was complicated for him. They may not have been entirely ready to accept this newly dependable person, this son and brother who had roamed far from them and only recently returned.

My mom said she was just a child when she first saw my dad. What she saw was a boy who refused to get off horseback. In fact, if he returned home from somewhere on his horse, who by then might be winded and perspiring, he would dismount, scrounge for something to fill his empty stomach, then hoist himself back onto the horse to eat. She said his mother would be cursing angrily, but every time she got close, he backed up suddenly and the horse sprang away, always out of her reach. Only at nightfall was he caught, when he failed to see his older sister Sadie's stealthy approach and the arm that yanked at him until he fell and lay at the hooves of his four-legged companion. Could my *Nali* and Aunt Sadie now accept this new, mature son and brother? Did my dad accept his new role of attentive father and husband? Powerful matriarchs encourage us to improve and refine our character, but if they are overly critical, they may not see or accept the changes we make. I can't recall ever hearing my *Nalí* say *Nizhoni*, or *You did that beautifully*. My *Ma Sani*, on the other hand, often praised my efforts, making me want to earn more of her accolades.

Another matriarch came into my life when I officially became a fourth grader. Mrs. O'Conner was tall and thin, with glasses and an Eleanor Roosevelt style about her. Her toothy smile, drive, and constancy made me feel safe in her presence. She was a no-nonsense person. She didn't ask, *Is that a good idea?* to allow for self-reflection or correction. Nope. She got right to the point. *I don't think that's a good idea*. Or, *That's not acceptable*.

Teachers have plans, goals, and dreams, which become lessons and projects, selections for readings and activities. Mrs. O'Conner took that first day by storm. No question that we were in her fold. From her hair to her hands, her energy never quit. Her hair was streaked white on top, reminding me of a thunderbolt, then descended into a mixture of black and white, until at the base of her skull, close to her ears and neck, the hair was dark and vibrant. She arranged her hair in a bouffant, and the salt and pepper crowning her head misled me into believing she was much older than she really was. She was tall like Mrs. Querry, but her voice was clear and resonant. Little Mirror Manny and Jessie were not in my class, but if they had been they might have been deterred from their antics. We all sat at our desks with our hands folded, ready to spring into action.

Class. Boys and girls. Then Mrs. O'Conner explained, smiling, *I will call you boys and girls when I address you as a class, but I will know your names by the end of the day.* She did. It was hard not to be in awe of her confidence.

Mrs. O'Conner's spare frame dictated that her dresses hung loosely on her, but she belted them, accentuating her commanding height. She and Mrs. Querry must have shopped in the same shoe store because they wore similar sensible granny shoes, low heels, leather lace-ups. Their shoes were a version of Oxfords that I called *teacher shoes* for many years. And her hands—they had a life of their own. Never did I observe them hanging limp by her side. Like birds, they were in constant flight. When she became excited, our teacher waved, gesticulated, and rapidly scrawled information on the chalkboard, tilting her head and reading aloud as she wrote. When she sought to make a point related to size, she stretched her arms wide open. From my fourth-grade perspective, her arm span was continent-wide. I imagined she could stride across Tennessee in the morning and be present to escort us out of school at dismissal time. When she assigned homework on that first day, she said, *Boys and girls, I want to see you place your assignment in that special place in your folder for homework. You may show me now as I inspect.* Who could fool around with that kind of authority? I liked Mrs. O'Conner, but I would be very careful not to get on her bad side.

The first day of class, Mrs. O'Conner arranged our desks in rows facing the blackboard. Behind us was a wall of tall windows that allowed us to see into an empty courtyard. Thanks to these windows, our room was bright with natural light. The morning sun shone in, but even in the afternoon heat our classroom remained cool, likely the result of a fan I now associate with swamp coolers. When I stepped into the entrance of Garfield's wide brick building, the corridors echoed, and I was bathed in cool air. Garfield's floors were wooden and its ceiling high. Whereas Rio Vista Elementary was a modern structure, Garfield was a historic building; its early twentieth century architecture possessed a grandeur driven by hopeful planners. In fact, when I later read *To Kill a Mockingbird*, Scout's school house was already familiar to me. It was Garfield Elementary. The tall windows reminded us we were confined, but just on the other side of those beautiful windows was more beauty, the beauty of freedom. Later I would learn that the courtyard beyond the windows encompassed our walkway to the restrooms, although I never once slowed to a walk during lunch. To me, the restroom was a brief intermission that I sped to and from, reluctant to miss a single minute of play. I gazed out of our classroom windows if I happened to sharpen my pencil or retrieve a book from the adjacent shelf. However, there was not much idle gazing under Mrs. O'Conner's supervision.

Soon we received our textbooks. We copied math problems onto paper to review skills we had likely forgotten over the summer. We read aloud to demonstrate our abilities and enthusiasm. We also practiced cursive. As I wrote in my best hand, I remembered Alfred from Rio Vista with his much praised, perfect letters. I was less anxious about my letters now because I wasn't driven by love for Mrs. O'Conner as I had been for Mrs. Monroe. Nothing came close to the wonders of Mrs. Monroe's teaching, but Mrs. O'Conner had her own style, which I adapted to and came to appreciate.

When we read aloud in Mrs. O'Conner's class, she stopped us to ask questions. Periodically, we obediently took out a sheet of paper and wrote a half-page about a theme. *Only a half page*, she stressed. When we finished, we read more of the text aloud. Mrs. O'Conner asked us how we felt now that we had moved further into the plot. Then we were assigned a partner with whom we read and wrote corrections on the half-page. I was glad to get to know my peers, but I was even happier to realize that with time to reflect on

Mrs. O'Conner's questions, I was able to make better decisions about a plot or character predicament. I was learning. I began to see my dad's influence, his temperament mirrored in me: I made quick decisions, but with time, I might revisit them and make changes. The sequence of my judgments might go something like this: *Bad. He's a terrible person. May the Lord forsake him. Oh wait. Let's think about this some more. Poor bastard. God help him. He deserves our pity.*

In addition to the skills and knowledge I learned from Mrs. O'Conner, it was in her class that I began to understand the importance of my other teachers, my peers. There was Genevieve, Norma, Joy, Brian, Charlotte, Carla, Fria, Winnie, Serabella, Lucy, and Dorene. All outstanding in their own ways when I reflect on their impact. Fourth grade showed me how important other students were, as peers and as educators—of reading, arithmetic, speech—and how they nurtured my education and personal development. Even now, I replay small, cherished details that I recall about my peers, who occupy an almost sacred place in my memories of that year. My peer-educators were the broad, expansive board upon which Mrs. O'Conner wrote. These elementary students loom larger today than the students I encountered much later in high school.

Genevieve's folks owned a small neighborhood market north of Garfield. Their daughter was by far the best reader in the school. With her hair pulled neatly back in a tie and her favorite solid red oxford shirt, nothing ruffled her. She seemed to be guided by greater goals or forces. Like me, she loved to draw, but unlike me, she drew with mathematical precision. When I was placed in a large, advanced math class, she and I sat at a table in the back where, underneath her math work, she drew pictures of pretty girls in elaborate gowns. Like me, she used lined paper, gazing past the faint blue lines as she sketched princesses that she handed out for others to color before the day was over.

Norma was the second-best reader. While Genevieve was a shorty like me, her friend Norma was willowy tall. I suspect she and Genevieve had been friends since kindergarten, but then Norma sprouted like wheat, developing a stoop by fourth grade. Ever so kind, Norma never criticized anyone. She listened patiently and smiled, a faraway look in her blue eyes as she spoke. She was the perfect student to ask about a good book; she and Genevieve would invariably have read more than anyone else by the end of the year. I was envious, but also awed and proud because they were my classmates. By the time I met Norma, she was re-reading books she liked. Long before book club meetings were born, Norma shared her very reliable recommendations with me.

Like Norma, blonde Joy was kind. On the playground she counterbalanced my fast and furious motions. If I wanted to unwind before the bell rang, I would find Joy on the swings. She was my cool-down companion. She might ask thoughtfully, *How's your day, Evelyn? What did you think of ...?* referring to class. While the student population was largely Latino, Joy didn't seem to register even a hint of conflict. Her caring spirit was one source of her composure, but I could also tell that she carefully observed her peers' habits. She phrased her observations with care: *Carlos is really good at paper airplanes. I'm gonna ask him to show me how to make one, so I can teach my little brother.* Or, *I wonder if I could get Carlos to make me three paper airplanes for my little brother.* She modeled the cool elder sister I had little interest in becoming. However, in the process, she invited camaraderie in Carlos by revealing his previously unnoticed paper airplane expertise. I bet Joy would have made a great teacher or psychologist.

Brian was Native, although I have no idea what his tribe was. He was a happy boy who I sometimes chased on the schoolyard. Like me, he made the most of after-lunch recess. I had a brief crush on him, but Mrs. O'Conner quickly extinguished that flicker by broadcasting it. What shame I must have felt to stop my Brian-chasing in my tracks. Was it how I felt my secrecy revealed to the light of day that made me retreat to my seat?

Charlotte was my best friend. She was Navajo, but she didn't speak the language. When I forgot that and broke out in Navajo, she looked at me reproachfully. *You know I can't speak it.* Fortunately, she was quick to forgive and was soon back to her pleasant self. With her I could relax my guard, giggling at nothing at all. I recall the two of us standing at the corner of Garfield and Twelfth Street laughing until our tears ran. What set us off? Who knows? Perhaps in laughter we found an antidote to the baffling moments of our home lives, just as we both found solace in books that we shared and escaped into. *Tell me when you're done so I can check it out after you* bound us together. If I liked a book, she accompanied me when I checked it in. The librarian called us *the reading friends.*

By contrast, Carla found her way into my fourth-grade life by virtue of her very large snake. One day her mother came to our class and out of her inconspicuous black leather bag she pulled a snake. How a writhing, slithering, bridge cable-thick snake could nestle in the bag, I couldn't fathom. While some Navajo traditions and practices made little sense to me, I never argued with the taboo of snakes. They horrified me. So when Carla said her snake was still growing, I saw gruesome images of the snake opening its jaws and devouring Carla's or a younger sibling's hand or foot. I was relieved to know that Carla didn't live anywhere near me. One day I asked her about her snake, and to my horror, she said it had somehow escaped. They searched and searched but it was never found. After that, whenever I saw a picture of a python or boa constrictor, Carla's snake took on the hideous proportions of these serpents. The lost snake made me overly cautious for what seemed like ages. I checked my bedding before crawling in and peered into the dense tangles of oleanders when I walked by. I felt a surge of revulsion when I saw black leather bags, which seemed to contain the same dangers as my gargoyles and leviathans.

Fria lived on Ninth Street. She was the reigning young beauty queen. Her appeal was intensified by an edginess about her that I didn't understand or trust. A bright student, she always looked like she was bored with knowledge. I was the exact opposite, which may be why I was drawn to her.

Who didn't love Winnie? She had a slight lisp, but that didn't keep her from talking with everyone, boy or girl. Her self-deprecating humor always made me smile. *Oh, you mean I shouldn't do that? What about this?* She had a loud and contagious laugh, and I sometimes heard her before I saw her. Mondays weren't Mondays without Winnie. When I said, *See you on Monday, Winnie,* I meant every word of it. She built up my confidence in my English and was the first person to detect my sense of humor. Though I had never met Winnie's mother, I liked her because she allowed Winnie to wear shorts to school. Winnie was a tall, muscular Black girl, but her voice seemed to emanate from someone much smaller and unassuming. Her routine attire of shorts and skirts suggested pure athleticism, but Winnie asserted her feminine side as well. She changed her earrings often and wore colorful barrettes and ribbons. I loved how she defied stereotypes. She openly admired certain boys, and from her I learned that liking a boy was just that, liking him. There was no shame in unreciprocated affection. I had had my Denny Garcia experience in second grade, but when Winnie told Juan, *You're cute, Juan,* and followed up with a friendly smile and laugh, she wasn't asking for Juan to return her feelings but merely expressing a truth. She didn't let her emotions get the better of her. I could have used her fourth-grade wisdom a lot later in high school.

Serious Serabella had dazzling dark skin, and her eyes were narrow, like mine. She was the first person who announced and demonstrated her deep connection with her faith. By then I had seen the kissing of crosses on necklaces or seeing them adorn on not-so-nice people. By contrast, Serabella was an altogether different fabric of worship. She was miles ahead of us in self-control, observing her faith with quiet commitment. When we practiced for the Christmas program, singing holiday songs, she opted out of this shallow pageantry. Her faith surpassed our bouncy tunes, going beyond into the ether. I liked the fact that Mrs. O'Conner never mentioned Serabella's faith or questioned her refusal to participate in activities, which had the unintended effect of imbuing her with an aura of mystery. While we toiled in practice, singing songs that didn't make any sense, Serabella read or studied elsewhere. I referred to her when I was grappling with my faith at a much later time.

I usually walked home with Charlotte along Garfield Street until we parted at Eleventh Street, where she would backtrack to McKinley and Twelfth. Sometimes Lucy walked with us. A science buff, all Lucy wanted to talk about was science trivia or experiments she had discovered. *Hey, have you ever added baking soda to a glass of Coke? Watch out! Did you know air pressure changes depending on the temperature?* Lucy weighed everything and asked endless questions. The tip of her tongue skated back and forth along her upper lip as she analyzed information. She read the science sections of *The Weekly Reader* muttering, *Cool. This is so cool*, and reported to us on recent scientific events in a way that showed her comfort with the language of science. From Lucy, I learned to use openers like *Research shows* as a way to end a dispute. Mainly I became fascinated with discovery. Lucy's constant questions reduced science to understandable terms by applying it to real life. I realized that topics of investigation were everywhere—from the kitchen to the bathroom to the sidewalk. *I wonder how a pickle tastes with red chili? Is a bath better than a shower? Can a 10-speed go faster than 10 miles per hour?* Lucy speculated on questions that I later explored. She fried an egg on the sidewalk and sizzled one with a magnifying glass. And all this took place near her front door because, like me, she had to take care of a younger sibling, in her case a little sister.

Most people I knew were good-hearted, but Dorene was on the top rung of that ladder. She reminded us, *That's not nice, you guys,* when we took things too far. *How nice* alerted us we were back in her good graces. She invariably spotted animals, mainly birds, to point out their beauty. If we read something about a bird, we all turned to Dorene to hear her *Oh, so cute* expression before proceeding. Dorene wore a perpetual smile. Once when I saw her cry about something, I felt oddly shaken, as though whoever or whatever had hurt her had broken an unspoken law. Those as kind as Dorene should be exempt from pain.

There were others, but these students live most vividly in my memory, forever fourth graders. I would move to Emerson Elementary the following year, where I expected to reunite with some of my fourth-grade comrades but didn't. Later, several of my former peers attended North High School, while others, like me, would attend Phoenix Union

High School, less than a mile west of Garfield. My neighborhood was in a crosswind of schools. This became a family discussion topic as I proceeded through fourth grade. For now, I was safely tucked under the watchful eyes of Mrs. O'Conner.

When Mrs. O'Conner broached the subject of math, I was all ears. Aside from the hiccup in Mrs. Querry's class, I was happy to be in math. After we received our math books, I surveyed the text from cover to cover, beginning with the table of contents, then flipping through chapters with new terms I couldn't pronounce. I studied examples of problems and the steps to solving them. As I read each step, I imagined I heard a tiny voice directing me. When I finished my survey, I rewarded myself by turning to a random page to preview solutions. I was seeing into the future, eager for a hint of the kinds of problems I would encounter later that year.

Mrs. O'Conner also distributed a new orange-colored vocabulary series. Though it was slim, I could see we would learn scores of new words this year. We practiced rote memory drills, copying ten words on paper and writing the words five times in cursive. Our pretest was Thursday morning when Mrs. O'Conner handed out loose-leaf newsprint paper cut vertically. She pronounced the words, and we spelled them. Then we switched papers. With a pen or colored pencil, we checked them and signed at the bottom. Mrs. O'Conner let us use our spelling books to check the work. She collected only perfect one hundred percent papers. The rest knew which words to practice for Friday's test, which everyone, even one hundred percenters, would take. *Another opportunity to knock my socks off, class.* Mrs. O'Conner gave us time to write our words before moving on to another subject. The beauty of this method was that if we earned a perfect score, we had free time, not long, but long enough for Genevieve to draw a princess and for me to thumb through the next set of vocabulary words. That was a better reward for me than the one hundred percent.

On Friday Mrs. O'Conner administered the same test, but this time she collected all the papers. We got results that afternoon, leaving school with our graded tests in hand to show our folks. My dad, in a hurry to shower and clean up, merely called out to my mom asking brusquely how we behaved that day and whether we had done our homework. It was my mom who was the engineer and conductor of our education train. Each week, after seeing my perfect scores, she asked to see the spelling words on what she called my *skinny paper*. Although she couldn't read or write, she could detect confidence in my writing, and she used my lack of erasures on the thin newsprint as evidence of my academic progress. I was already seeing that some of my classmates were less enthusiastic than I was about school, and I still wonder what part my mom's vigilance played in my love of learning.

These weekly spelling tests were stressful, so a few of us practiced outside before the morning bell or as we walked home. I memorized new words by using my finger to trace their letters in the air. I found methods for memorization intuitively, adopting them to my language habits. My dad sometimes modeled the finger movements, motivating my desperate efforts to spell the words correctly. I would often find myself motioning with my index finger, depending on muscle memory for accuracy. My method had its limits, apparently. To this day, I have trouble with certain words. *Icy, scary, gauge,* and *postpone* elude me. I want to add an /ey/ to *icy* and *scary*. I pronounce *postpone* as *postphone*. And of course, if I mispronounce a new word, I'm sure to misspell it. Spelling in isolation had its limits, but I learned to memorize, and I often spelled words aloud with friends when I could have been playing on the monkey bars. Despite challenges, I learned many words in fourth grade under the scrutiny of Mrs. O'Conner. Her energy was contagious. It just took some time to adjust.

One unmistakable contrast between third and fourth grade was the absence of our mid-morning break. We had lunch followed by fun and games at midday, but where was earlier recess? I felt cheated, as though the school was reneging on an agreement that compensated for the long, strenuous day. Morning recess was part bribery, part escape, and a much-needed release from being stuck at a desk. In fact, when Mrs. O'Conner went over the schedule on the first day of school, I was sure that she'd made an error by not mentioning morning recess. When she failed to bring it up the second day, I knew something was terribly wrong. I looked around at my classmates, but no one seemed concerned. They were like leaves in the breeze, fluttering onto the next topic with Mrs. O'Conner.

Chapter 5 - Fourth Grade: Train and Boxcars Journey

I raised my hand to speak. Later I would put names to the faces staring at me, but on the second day of school, so many heads turned in my direction shook my confidence.

Mrs. O'Conner, did we forget to have recess yesterday? I asked in a quivering voice.

Mrs. O'Conner looked like she was taken by surprise. Her bird-like hands were still. *Why no, Evelyn. Fourth graders do not have recess. Fourth graders are too big for recess.*

I struggled to comprehend this. It was as though my command of English had evaporated. I heard *Fourth graders*. Yes, I was a fourth grader, but I didn't understand what being *too big for recess* meant. I certainly wasn't too big. I loved it like I loved the rest of school.

I'm sorry, she said. *We have too much to do this year for recess.*

Not expecting this response, I abandoned whatever dignity I had and let one fat tear escape. Once the dam broke in one place, the rest collapsed quickly, sobs following the trail of the first. Tears splattered, and I shook so hard that Mrs. O'Conner hurried over to hold me. Somewhere she found a handkerchief to wipe my face. She must have been affected, because she used another corner of her white handkerchief to dab her own eyes,

But why? I sobbed as she held me. Being in her warm presence brought relief in a new surge of hot tears. My tears surprised me. They certainly surprised Mrs. O'Conner. The class had a mixed reaction, with expressions ranging from *Crybaby Evelyn* to *Use those tears. Work it, girl.* A student turned to wink at me, as though I had fulfilled my role in some hidden pact. Mrs. O'Conner seemed uncertain and bought some time by launching into a description of our next class project, the Reading Train.

Despite my tears, I felt myself scrambling back onto her band wagon. She was enthusiastically waving colorful construction paper boxcars in the air, each of which, she informed us, would represent a completed book. Then she pointed to the black locomotive and engine, already tacked to our class wall, but in her was the caboose. *We will build our reading train boxcar by boxcar. For every book you finish, you will label a boxcar with the title of your book, the author, the publication date, the genre, and your rating of one to five stars. Your name will be on the back.* Clearly Mrs. O'Conner was taken with this project because she led us out into the corridor and pointed to the wall where the train would forge a path. When we reached the entrance of the restrooms, she said, *Our train will break here but will continue on,* as we followed her down the echo-y hallway. *By the end of the year, we want to display our caboose inside our library.* We trailed after her beckoning arms until we reached the library, where we filed inside, by now inspired to get our train moving. A few cocky students whispered about choosing short books or books they had already read. If Mrs. O'Conner heard them, she didn't let on. She had successfully averted a disaster over recess, and now avoided another derailment with her reading project. I was already off looking for any *Betsy* books I might have missed at Rio Vista. We were eating right out of her hands, like small, grateful, hungry birds.

As we hung on Mrs. O'Conner's words about the reading train, I guessed how many books we would need to read to reach the library. I was excited to be part of a whole society of readers setting off on a journey. The number of books didn't phase me; I was just thrilled to join in the reading train community. I saw it as a global adventure, traveling to distant places and into unknown lives, yet safe and secure in the role of reader. Our librarian shared her newest additions to the library, and students flocked to see these titles. I was still too shy from my teary display to join them, but I was comforted by their smiles and mild jostling as they reached for the books.

Oh, Evelyn. You are right near the section I want to show you. With that, Mrs. O'Conner introduced me to Beverly Cleary, and my rapid migration to her from Carolyn Haywood was like hitting an instant jackpot. This is not to say that recess had loosened its grip on me, as the book train was in addition to, not instead of the playground.

When we returned to the classroom, Mrs. O'Conner said a few words more about our project, then followed up with, *Let's get familiar with our new books and see what happens after fifteen minutes.* I wasn't entirely sure what she meant because I was already cracking open my *Ramona Quimby*, but when I saw others smiling gleefully, I guessed her meaning.

So that's how we won an occasional recess. We agreed to all sorts of rules in exchange for freedom beneath the rays of the sun. We limited ourselves to the green and the swings and the teeter totter section. It didn't matter that we would later walk home under the same sky, in the same heat. It was the principle—sweet release from the classroom. During this short reprieve, we played a version of musical chairs, but in this version, we simply froze in our tracks when we heard Mrs. O'Conner's whistle. With her whistle clasped between her lips as she walked, she never failed to surprise us with the shrill signal to halt. She laughed at the poses we struck in mid-movement, at least those of us who didn't fall down. Those who lost their balance were out. Eventually we were reduced to five or six on the greens. Then the inevitable final whistle herded us back to the cool classroom.

Fourth grade introduced another milestone: physical education. I believe it was meant to replace the wild, undisciplined chaos of recess. But while I loved jumping jacks, pull-ups, sit-ups, the toe touches, stretches, and scrimmages, recess held me in its nostalgic El Monte embrace, reconnecting me to my first friend Becky while keeping at bay my awareness that I was growing up. Recess let me take brief refuge in childhood. I was well-aware that not everyone enjoyed it as much as I did. Some girls were already strolling in pairs or lounging in the shade waiting for the signal back to the classroom.

That same watershed year, I discovered the *Little House on the Prairie* book series. I vacillated between modern, irreverent Ramona's world on one hand and Laura's life on the frontier on the other. While I knew that neither of these series acknowledged my culture except to ignore us or subject us to rampages, I still cherished the stories.

One weekend around that time, my family had a burglary at our house on East Roosevelt. We happened to be away at one of our weekend getaways to the White House. Oddly, the thieves only took my mom's LP collections. Some LPs were taken while their cardboard sleeves were left behind. We had a modest household, so beyond a few tools, some clothing, and crockery, nothing excited the thieves beyond the record albums, a Pendleton blanket, and our new colored TV.

My dad had started spending time with our Navajo next-door neighbors Tommy and Bella. When I stepped out into the yard, Bella would call to me cheerfully as she washed dishes or puttered in her tiny kitchen space. Over time, I realized that many of the records Bella liked best were the ones that had disappeared. Making things worse, my dad, looking for good cheer, often drank with Tommy and Bella on weekends. At least we knew where he was at those times.

The LP theft might have been the last straw for my mom. She found another one-bedroom apartment for all of us, this one on Garfield and Eleventh Street, for $55 a month. The homes where we lived were, by necessity, always affordable. Rent on Jones Avenue was $45, Roosevelt was $56, and our new Garfield place was $55 a month. The highest rent my folks paid was $68 before we moved to New Mexico, but that was still six years in the future. This one-half bedroom house had a sizable porch, well-shaded by towering pecan trees, and a backyard where my dad parked his new-but-used 1967 blue Chevy long bed with a 283 V8 engine. Later my dad paid $99 to have the blue painted flaming orange. I was amazed that within a few days, a truck's exterior could be magically transformed and offer unknown possibilities. I associated that paint job with the move away from Tommy and Bella and my dad's sudden reawakening to his family duties. He was so unlike a popular handheld toy called Weebles Wobbles: Round-based Weebles tottered but they didn't land flat. He certainly fell, but my mom willingly picked him up again, and here he was in our midst, again. Our down-and-up dad.

I'm not sure which was worse, Tommy and Bella's betrayal or my dad's. My dad was doing a poor job of finding trustworthy friends, making honest use of his hard-earned income, making the most of our brief childhood, and repairing his frayed marriage. I sometimes peeked over the top of my book at my parents from my new bedroom as I worked or read. I was just beginning to see their flaws. They seemed like children at times, playing their blame games.

I recall the yellow walls of my new bedroom—really more an alcove than a room—where my twin-sized bed fit snugly against the walls. There was an ancient ceiling light fixture and a window that swung open to let in the cool air at night and in the early morning. I had screwed in a pencil sharpener that Dean and I loved to use. The apartment had a mini-kitchen and a large living room space with crown molding that I imagined some dreamer, a long-ago resident or landlord, might have added to beautify the room. I also liked the brown wooden floor, freshly painted before we moved in. It made sweeping easy when the fine grains hid between the cracks of the wood, and it was cool for my feet when I woke up early and padded to the window to admire the pecan trees. Our apartment was hidden in a block of homes, and the alley behind the back door was rarely used, so this was a perfect quiet nest for us.

This move brought me closer to Charlotte, whose family lived down the alley. Carla, the snake owner, also knew where we lived. In her opinion we were *dirty, lazy people*; proof was the location of our home. Not so for me. When I visited the homes of friends, I encountered the same crowded conditions: the smell of fried foods, couches with worn armrests, strategically placed throws to cover tired upholstery, and curled tiles below my feet. Since this was all I knew, I found these homes as familiar and comfortable as good home-cooking. There were some beautiful historic homes here and there, but apartments for $55 a month rarely materialized in expensive neighborhoods. Nevertheless, I can genuinely say we were cozy in our home.

Dean and I had our friends, our parents, our schools, and our teachers; we also had well-ingrained habits, like accepting the educational dogma that promised betterment. This had roots in our identity, language, and culture, and in our protective mother. Our dad's troubled youth had made him unsure of himself in some ways, but my mom knew exactly what she did and didn't want. She was absolutely sure about what she didn't want for Dean and me: the kind of alcoholic battles our father fought every weekend. Though she and our dad didn't argue around us, the tension was palpable. Thankfully, Dean and I had means of escape in reading and drawing.

I still wrote letters to my cousin-sister Venne about my reading, school, and friends, areas of my life that I treasured. My brother had art. My mom had her loom and when she needed a diversion from that, she beaded objects that she sold to shops. Sometimes she made me beaded leather barrettes or hair ties that I wore in my long braids.

That year, I quietly discovered an unlooked-for peril resulting my enthusiasm for math. I had just finished the easy section of some math problems at home, where I was lying belly-down on my bed. I checked my multiplication and was pleased to find that the answers were all correct. I was launching into the harder section, so to start fresh, I jumped up to sharpen my pencil. With my newly pointed pencil in hand, I leaped back on to the bed, expecting to land where my math book was propped open. My aim was good enough, but I punctured my inner eyelid when I landed, and though my eyeball was spared, I had to listen to the sickening suction of my skin releasing the pencil lead as I pulled it out. Not a fun moment. I didn't dare tell my parents because I certainly would have been threatened with a whupping on my behind. Instead, I went into the bathroom to examine a new grey shadow next to the white of my eye. The next time I got excited about working hard math problems, I sharpened my pencil and tossed it onto the bed before diving after it.

My love of art was as mighty as my love of math. My art supplies included anything I could find in thrift stores. Sometimes it was charcoal pencils, pastels, colored pencils, and occasionally colored pens. Once I found a used watercolor set. My dad still tried to furnished sketch pads, but the stretches between having and not having one increased. In those cases, like Genevieve, I used lined paper, but eventually even that had to be rationed. *Paper doesn't grow on trees. What am I? A money tree?* My dad was not creative when lecturing us about thrift. Chapter books had occasional illustrations, and I read enough to decide I liked sketches by Garth Williams. I copied pen and ink illustrations from my books and drew pictures based on my reading and brought to life by my imagination. I wasn't talented, but I enjoyed using pencils and pens to accompany my reading.

It was Dean who showed real talent. He drew castles, obscure houses that often reminded me of M.C. Escher's illustrations, twisted and shifting optical illusions. Like my mom, he leafed through *National Geographic* and architectural magazines. He somehow persuaded a teacher to lend him an art book that couldn't be found in our school library. He would look at a picture, then render it on paper. He drew, he painted, and when he learned about origami, he took off on that. With a few sheets of construction paper and glue, he formed palaces and Victorian style houses. He checked out big books on architecture and design. At eight years old, he decided Art Deco was his favorite style. He was mad about anything related to Egyptian art: gods, pyramids, hieroglyphs, furnishings and the afterlife effects found in burial rooms. He added labels to his images, so his vocabulary increased at an amazing rate. Like Genevieve's friends, Dean's friends made special requests that he added to his homework load and distributed to his growing clientele before Friday dismissal. More than once, I heard him say, *Sorry Charlie, I can't do this week, but how about next week?* On Valentine's Day and Mother's Day, he was asked to draw bouquets of flowers. This wasn't his style, but he didn't mind the challenge of trying something new. It was hard to fault him.

Friday nights, when my dad was gone, my mom wove, and my brother and I drew. We were all lost in worlds that we knew and owned. When my dad came home late, he may not have realized that we were gradually moving away from him. My mom no longer hurried to make him a meal welcoming him home. More than once I heard, *We ate already.* My mom cooked and we ate what she made, wiping the plate clean with her naan-like bread. Spam, potatoes, green beans and corn with chili were common fare. I washed the iron skillet, the plates, and the utensils and put them away so the kitchen counter was clean. Then we stayed where we were to resume our creative projects. When my dad arrived, he might get a wayward *Hi Da*, but our greetings were limp and empty. He may or may not have understood that his straying had led to our growing contentment with one other. Solidarity was forming. When he called for me, I broke my concentration to glance at him but quickly returned to my book or my drawing. It wasn't exactly resentment that made me turn away, but I felt myself beginning to see him differently, and I was settling into my own separate world.

Not willing to accept this change, he wooed us with cajoling, laughter and bribery. He bought me a sketchpad and 64-Crayola box with a sharpener. I resisted sharing this with

Dean, and it took multiple threats of spankings from my mom before I relented. However, I took my Crayola box to school on the days I knew we would have art, carrying it home so my mom wouldn't detect my sly hoarding. I must have become too comfortable with my routine at school, because the one time I left it overnight in my desk, it was gone the next day. Trying not to give into desperation, I waited a whole 24 hours before reporting it to Mrs. O'Conner. She asked me to clean out my desk to be sure and told me to wait until the following day. The next day she said, *I'm sorry Evelyn, but I couldn't find it. It's a sad loss.* I stood still, taking in her words while hot tears began to form. I nodded and left class, walking home slowly as I told myself it was my fault for bringing the Crayolas to class. But no matter how I chided myself, I didn't feel the loss any less sharply.

It so happened that my dad noticed I was back to using my hodgepodge of art supplies and asked, *Where are your crayons?* I hadn't rehearsed a story, so I told him the truth. Once again tears flooded my eyes. It was partly regret for being selfish with the crayons and also for leaving them in the desk as temptation for others. I realized that I had expected my belongings to be as safe as I felt under Mrs. O'Conner's care.

My dad generally stayed out of squabbles between my brother and me, saying simply *Work it out.* However, this time he decided to act. Even as I narrated the story, I felt at fault, but my dad must have heard something else. He pulled out a paper and began to write, blowing on his fingers as he did when he composed. He signed and folded the letter into an envelope that I was to take to my teacher.

The next day, I solemnly placed the enclosed letter on her desk because my shame made it unbearable to stand near her. Later I observed that the letter was no longer on her desk, and I made sure not to arouse attention for the rest of the day. I never knew what was in the letter, but Mrs. O'Conner handed me a brand-new replacement set, saying only, *Keep it at home, Evelyn. Thank you.* Though delighted, I was still deeply ashamed when I took my new crayons home. I always blamed myself for losing them and unnecessarily bringing my dear teacher into this messy dilemma of my own making.

Sometime in mid-fall, I was transferred to Mrs. Peabody for math. Her room was across the corridor, but it was a different environment altogether. I entered the class shyly, not sure I wanted to leave Mrs. O'Conner's classroom. When I walked in, to my surprise I saw Genevieve, Norma, Dorene, Joy, and Winnie. All seats were occupied, so I joined Genevieve at a table in the back. Mrs. Peabody was young and knew her math. As she took attendance, she stopped and asked a student to recite the multiples of seven. Sandra stood up, and with quivering pig tails and fluttering eyes focused upward, she began, *Seven times one equals seven,* and on she went all the way to *seven times twelve*. My stomach tightened. I knew I wouldn't be in this new class for long if I couldn't stand and mimic Sandra and others. So in addition to my math homework, I began to shut myself in the family bathroom before the mirror to recite my multiples. I used the mirror to watch my mouth, discouraging stuttering by drawing out words that gave me trouble. I also used my exhalation to elongate certain words that wanted to stumble and trip. I devised this strategy on my own, and discovered, to my relief, that it worked.

Mrs. Peabody's teaching style was similar to Mrs. Monroe's, but her classroom didn't include any soft music in the background, nor did she require silent observation when she introduced a new math problem. While Mrs. Peabody intimidated some students, including me, I flourished under her instruction. Like many purposeful, confident teachers, she managed her class with queenly composure. She didn't smile much, and never laughed, but introduced us to a rigor that was necessary and welcome. Sometimes she allowed students to come in after school to retake tests. I felt I had a safety net under me if I needed it.

Mrs. Peabody stressed the importance of enunciation, posture, and eye contact. I saw students who slumped elsewhere sit up straight and add, *Yes m'am,* for good measure. I was glad to have been placed in her class, and though this was my first time in the "high group," I was like a duck returning to familiar waters, swimming quickly to join my siblings. I don't recall being corrected or singled out even when we were invited to show our homework on the board. I had felt secure in Mrs. Monroe's and Mrs. O'Conner's classes, but now I was meticulous about double-checking my calculations before volunteering an answer. If I was called on to answer, I did so thoughtfully as I stood to my full height with my arms and hands resting by my side, fingertips pressed into my thighs as I recited.

Perhaps with this newfound confidence, I joined an after-school program that could easily have been a version of Girl Scouts. Charlotte and I were assigned to be hall monitors, so we hurried to school a little early to put on our orange vests. We were to watch the north doors to keep students out of the building. If a student ignored our scripted speech: *I'm sorry but you can't come into the building until the first bell rings*, and walked past us, we reported him or her to the front office. I felt newly important in this role, almost like a grownup. Fourth grade was lightyears from adulthood, but since Garfield Elementary was a K-4 school, we fourth graders ruled the roost. We were the big kids, in our eyes just a short step away from teachers.

Besides Mrs. O'Conner, who we revered, another of our favorite teachers was Mrs. Green, our music teacher. Even before we transitioned to music, as we were putting away our books, we heard her wheeling her piano down the wooden-floored corridor, playing a refrain and singing along. The first time I heard her, I half-believed a circus had come to school and was heralding a parade of animals down the hall. What a delightful fright that was. When I couldn't contain myself and rose from my seat, I saw a gleaming brown piano on wheels being guided into the classroom. Mrs. O'Conner laughed and announced, *Look who's here, class!* closely followed by Mrs. Green. I wanted to assist, but I sat in the middle of the class. Lucky students who sat near the entrance helped guide Mrs. Green's piano into our space.

Mrs. Green beamed. Recently I'd learned, It's *a delight to make your acquaintance*, and she may have been the only person I would have said this to and meant it.

Mrs. Green introduced chords for songs we sang. We didn't have any material other than her piano and our voices. I can't recall whether Mrs. O'Conner slipped out or joined us for "She'll be Coming 'Round the Mountain," "This Land is Your Land," "Michael Row the Boat Ashore," "Oh Susannah," and "Kumbaya." These were glorious times of the week. Mrs. Green fluctuated between standing and stooping as she played, a beatific smile on her face. When she taught us a new song, she wrote the lyrics on the board, and then masterfully brought the piano to life again as we learned the song. She infused a new energy into our class, one that seemed to lift our mood and brighten the air itself. When our time together came to an end, Mrs. Green made a sad face and, with the help of two students, wheeled her piano out the door and into the hall. While she had appeared to be near tears as she exited our classroom, I could hear her exuberant, ringing voice as she entered another room. Mrs. Green had a larger-than-life quality, as though she inhabited an altogether different space than most of us. The result was her ability to inspire our pure joy in music and song.

Later in December, we joined Mrs. Green in the auditorium to learn Christmas carols. Aware that we had an audience of teachers slipping in and out of the auditorium, I sang in a voice I hardly knew but thought was my best. We created beautiful harmonies, some voices soaring as others descended, all coalescing into an actual chorus under the guidance of our teacher. We performed in a Christmas program that my mom attended, and for which I agreed to wear a dress.

At long last, my mom had relented and let me wear slacks or jeans to school without too much criticism. The first day I wore them, I felt like I had finally entered society. Even then, my mom sometimes sewed a new dress to tempt me. Girls occasionally boasted about sassing their mothers: *My mom can't tell me what to do*, but that wasn't me by any stretch. My mom was a powerhouse, and my parents exacted obedience from Dean and me. Now I wonder whether our very agreeable natures were not part of our effort to hold together a family that was steadily unraveling as our father drank and strayed more often.

Dean and I might have spilled into the Phoenix streets like many of our friends were it not for our mother. We regularly heard her at her loom, beating the dyed woolen yarn cleaned from a bundle given to her by my *Ma Sani*, who said, *You will make rugs with this*. *Ma Sani* smiled as she said to me, *Take care of this for your mom*. I couldn't bear to disappoint her. Her smile, and my sense of duty, were enough to ensure my cooperation. I could not imagine defying my *Ma Sani* or my mom.

I had won the war against dress-wearing thanks to the specter of Little Mirror Mario. Now I was developing another reason to shun dresses beyond comfort as I began to associate dresses with maternal responsibilities. By this time, I was perched on the highest rung at Garfield Elementary, and knew I would advance steadily and inevitably to high school. It seemed I was being prepared for murky adulthood. Wearing pants was a welcome reminder that I could slow the process. I could run, jump, race, and hurl my body against the future.

My next clothing wish was for overalls, which I envisioned myself wearing with one shoulder strap undone and pant cuffs rolled up. I had seen house painters in white overalls, and since I liked painting, I thought I should dress for the part. Other styles began to claim my attention. I loved cornrows. I tried braiding my hair tightly, but mine lacked the neatness of Winnie's. I turned away from the colorful ribbons my mom tied in my hair, though I continued to wear the beaded hair ties she made. I had two sets, one flaming orange and the other ocean blue glass. They were two and a half inches in diameter with a mandala-like design that was sewn to a leather backing with suede straps. Sometimes, so that I could look at the mesmerizing designs, I tied one to my wrist, like a watch. My mom's beadwork was a reminder of the power of art, Mrs. Monroe, and my Native-ness. My mom occasionally said, *This once girl is now a woman because she won't wear ribbons or let me fix her hair.* I shrugged off her criticism.

One day I was tucked into the swing on the playground, concentrating my legs and body to launch into the air, when a male passerby called out, *A baby. Look at the baby swing.* I wasn't sure how to take this. Yes, I loved to swing, but this taunt made me ashamed of my joy, so I slowed down and waited until he was gone before I continued my flight. Nothing was like soaring high up in the air with a view of Garfield that was invisible from the ground. Later, when I encountered palm tree trimmers in my neighborhood, I stopped and looked at their harnesses and the spiked grips on their shoes as they jimmied up palm trunks. I decided I wanted to do that when I was older because then I could see all around the neighborhood. It remained a secret wish because my parents would have laughed at me.

In the spring, students were corralled into a small auditorium where we watched a ballet performance. A man and woman in tights and fancy costumes danced for us, and while I had no idea what we were watching, the dancers' graceful movements set to classical music introduce me to another form of performance art. With its leaps and turns in the air, the performance was not quite the same as Pinocchio, but I liked it. We clapped loudly and someone in the front yelled, *Encore!* Others joined, and then the couple returned to the stage. The ballerina spun, and when she slowed down, her partner caught her and held her with one arm as she bent backwards. I was amazed that dancing for an audience could be an actual occupation. When we left the auditorium, I happened to be behind my classmate Juanito. He peered into a small window in the door and motioned for me to join him, where I saw the two ballet dancers in an embrace. This struck Juanito's funny bone, but not mine. I was puzzled and annoyed, wondering whether their kiss somehow made their performance fake. I had imagined that the man and woman were in love with ballet, not with each other. I thought they'd wanted to share their art with us, public school kids, and I felt cheated. The backstage embrace also reminded me that girls, including me, would transform one day. Our bodies would change, and I wondered if I would ever want an embrace like the one I had just seen. I also wondered if Juanito would still laugh about this sight in the not-so-distant future.

Later in the same spring of 1974, my dad's older brother, Uncle Kee Nez, came to visit. He wanted to relocate to Phoenix, so he stayed with us until he found work and rented a place. Years before, Uncle Kee Nez had served in the Vietnam War. During his service he regularly sent money to my *Nali*, and out of this war pay, she gave my dad money for my baby formula. My mom reminded me of his sacrifice, so I practiced good manners, but he was simply another adult to me at the time. He had little interest in children. He was an adult who drew and painted, boxed and rodeoed. I couldn't know then that he and I would develop a friendship after I returned to Phoenix. But at this time, he was simply a distant figure to whom I knew I was indebted.

My uncle woke up early, and sometimes he was shirtless. I'm sure the Phoenix heat was unbearable for him, and I don't recall a swamp cooler in our Garfield house. My mom enjoyed anyone who complimented her cooking. I recall her serving him a big breakfast, repeatedly putting food on his plate until he finally said, No *more please. I can't do it*, in Navajo. It was funny to watch a grown man struggle to make himself understood. Our family had developed our own traditions from our years in California and now in Phoenix. We spoke Navajo, abbreviating certain words that only we seemed to understand. Dean and I weren't shy about reverting to our Navajo in public. We always spoke in our first language when we were with our mom, but translating for her. We got straight to the point in our Navajo, unlike more formal, polite speakers.

My Uncle Kee Nez was amused by Dean and me. Sometimes he found me outside on the porch engrossed in a book. I was keen on getting our class train into the library. On most Mondays, I asked for a construction paper boxcar to fill out the details of my newly finished book. I left this with Mrs. O'Conner, and later when I walked to the restroom, I made a detour to locate my boxcar on the wall.

After my uncle's day-long job search, he came back to us, showered, and cleaned up. Then he pulled a chair outside to keep me company. Like me, he noticed how peaceful it was, shaded by the awning of the porch. Next to us were two pecan trees, so tall that when I stood by the front door, I couldn't see the upper branches of the trees. A breeze stirred the leaves, which clattered softly, and even with some neighborhood traffic and children out playing, I found it a calm, quiet place to sit.

While I drew or read, Dean played with his friend Ron. Like us, Ron was on a short leash, responding right away when his grandmother called him. He lived next door behind a high cinderblock wall. Nikos, a neighbor my age who lived along Eleventh Street, sometimes came over to climb the pecan tree next to our apartment. Nikos was a reader, too, so he perched himself on a branch, then pulled out the book that was tucked inside his shirt. Sometimes he asked friendly questions, but when my uncle was nearby, I was shy. Occasionally Nikos threw me a piece of wrapped gum, or I threw an apple up to him. The previous autumn, he and his brother Demitrius had climbed this same tree to help harvest the pecans. We divided bags, and they took their share home to their grandmother. I was conscious of how easy it was to like and admire Nikos. He scurried up the pecan tree effortlessly, where he camped out to read. As soon as his grandmother called his name, he swung down and landed a few feet from the tree, tossing a *So long, Evelyn* over his shoulder. I acknowledged with my *See you, Nikos*.

Eventually my uncle found a job and an apartment. He struggled with alcoholism, but while he had stayed with us, my dad conducted himself like a model citizen. Arriving home from work, having dinner, then reading, my dad played his role with conviction. Kee Nez was his older brother, and I believe my dad wanted to set a good example for him. At this time, my uncle still suffered from nightmares from the war. My mom explained to us that the war had caused a hidden pain that emerged at night from the deepest of sleep. One day when I came home, my uncle had found my sketchpad. Mindful of good manners, I offered him my ragtag art set to use. Beyond his gift as an artist, he drew to relieve his sadness. His own family, as well as my mother, observed that his service had transformed him. My mom said, *Some should never serve because the changes scar gentlemen like Uncle Kee Nez.* One characteristic that didn't change was his ability to lose himself in drawing. He drew western scenes, gun fights, bucking horses, and cowboys riding into the sunsets. Later I saw the works of Frederic Remington and was reminded of my uncle's style and themes. He couldn't resist a blank white page. If he was home on a Saturday, he sat on that chair outside and drew and drew, using my sketchpad. On those days I read.

My Uncle Kee Nez had the first tattoo I ever saw up close. He also had a bone protruding from his shoulder. It was like seeing my dad's ugly injured foot but worse; I couldn't impolitely stare at it, much less ask questions about it. My mom didn't know how he had gotten his injury, but she chalked it up to rodeo. *He's lucky that's the only injury he walked away with*, she remarked, in a way that puzzled me. There were other things that I didn't understand about my uncle, but when he silently studied designs of the light filtering through the pecan leaves and branches, or his interest in the lines of the identical buildings in our small area—six apartment buildings connected with a narrow sidewalk—I understood him. He was introspective, like me, and I felt self-conscious around him probably because of our fascination with angles, curvatures, planes, and the arrays of light.

Sometimes my uncle took long walks with Dean, and when they returned, Dean had a sweet treat with him. Dean said they walked past Edison School to the east, or they walked past Emerson School to the north. My uncle, in his cowboy boots and worn Wranglers, managed these excursions better than my brother. Dean liked his sweets, but the explorations seemed to exhaust him. The walks might also have been a way for my uncle to accustom himself to our neighborhood. Coming from the high desert plains, he had often ridden horseback under the endless skies, so this new concrete setting with palm trees and incessant traffic must have been unsettling.

Before summer, my mom bought me strappy white sandals with flat heels. The straps dug into the outsides of my feet. I hated them because they looked like grown women sandals. What was wrong with thongs, what we now call flip flops? Everyone wore them, probably enjoying the sharp flapping sound against their heels. I wore the sandals daily and beat them up running, playing kick the can, climbing fences, and scrambling up trees. By midsummer, I noticed with satisfaction that two straps had pulled loose from the soles. The white color had grayed and been scratched off the surface of the patent leather. I got another *Doo baa aholya* about my beat-up pretty shoes. I tried to look remorseful, but my mom saw through my charade. Sockless, I quickly slipped on my Keds and hurried outside.

Charlotte's family lived at 1134 East McKinley in a clapboard rental house out in back, next to an alley. She had two older brothers who played chess and when they wanted a break, they sent Charlotte to ask my mom if Dean and I could play outside. We were all Navajo. Our outdoor games were brief, thanks to limited hiding spaces. Next to Charlotte's house was a two-story apartment. I noticed that Charlotte's older brothers did not invite the brother and sister, close in age to them, who lived there. I often glanced up at them as they leaned out the window of the apartment. Sometimes they revealed our hiding places, or yelled, *Watch out! Here comes Edwin!* They interfered repeatedly but we still played. Since the brother and sister were older, I didn't speak to them. They seemed to enjoy altering the course of the game. During a quiet moment, Charlotte whispered, *Those kids are Hopi.* I had no idea whether this was true or was the reason they didn't join us, but I eyed them when they weren't looking. I didn't know any Hopis, though I knew that many lived in Tuba City. Later, when summer arrived, as Charlotte and Edwin were walking us home after playing kick the can, I strode past the sister, and without a word, she yanked my hair so quickly and fiercely that I could feel my neck pop, like knuckles cracking. I was mystified. Charlotte must have noticed because she slipped her hand in mine. My scalp hurt but my ego hurt more.

That boarding-school moment warned me that fifth grade might be very different from fourth. Certainly, it proved true for Charlotte and me. Before school ended, she whispered sadly that her family would move to Northern Avenue, too far away for me to walk to see her. Charlotte's dad came to visit my parents to tell them the landlord wanted another Navajo family to move in when they vacated. We knew then where our next home would be in the early part of summer.

I was less certain about my future school. Nikos and Demetrius attended Emerson Elementary and liked it, but Nikos and his older brother represented a small sample. Emerson was farther away than Edison. To get there, I would walk through four blocks of neighborhood with even sidewalks, then past Good Samaritan Hospital, across McDowell Road, and three more blocks to a historic district. By the time I reached Emerson, neighborhood lawns were manicured, and houses seemed neat and polished. The asphalt was even, and people parked their cars in driveways or hugged close to the curb, yet still the streets had a spacious feel, trimmed with grass right up the sidewalks. The decision was easy for my folks; I would hoof the extra distance to Emerson Elementary.

At the end of the school year, I surveyed where my friends would go. Some were sure of Edison or Emerson while others were unsure. I assumed I would see my friends again at Emerson, but I didn't. Some I didn't see until high school, and some I never saw again. I had imagined I would see them scattered throughout the neighborhood over time, but I didn't yet understand how people would come and go, enter my sphere and vanish from it.

As I grew, my mom patched the knees and the seat of my jeans, and when they became too short, the hems flapping above my ankles, she reached for her scissors to cut off the legs at the knees. I also asked my mom to trim my hair, but she wouldn't, so I walked away muttering, *Then I'll cut it myself.* Aware of my determination, she agreed to trim two inches, and I felt a lighter load on my head. I was free.

Our class train had reached the library, and we followed the box cars along the hallway recounting our journey aloud. A photograph would have revealed a group of beaming fourth graders, delighted with our accomplishment. A few days later, Mrs. O'Conner returned the boxcars to each of us. I arranged mine in various orders: chronologically, alphabetically, and by my favorite reads. Beverly Clearly and Laura Ingalls Wilder were always close to the top.

Near the end of the year, I helped Mrs. O'Conner carry her classroom supplies to her red truck. It had a camper, so I was now the proud possessor of the fact that my teacher liked camping. The rear of her camper displayed all sorts of state stickers. I saw Alaska, New York, Minnesota, Montana, Wyoming, New Mexico, Florida, Pennsylvania, Virginia, and West Virginia. *Did you go to all those places, Mrs. O'Conner?* I asked her. Yes, she said. I was silent as I tried to imagine what these far-off lands were like. Pennsylvania stood out. *I had a teacher from Pennsylvania,* I said in an off-hand way. The end of our time together was near, and I felt that I was already saying good-bye.

You will go there one day and probably farther, Evelyn.

CHAPTER 6
Fifth Grade: Loss and Learning

Mr. Knight was my second male teacher. He was an older gentleman. He was on the tall side and he had a paunch. It was 1974. I knew very few heavy-set people, yet we called one another *Fatty* or *Fatso*, in a light-hearted manner, the awful way friends spoke to one another, taking friendships for granted. We wouldn't have extended our fun and games to Mr. Knight. He was far from our world. He wore a starched button-down shirt with a tie and his slacks was belted. He wore wingtips. He jingled his coins as he walked. He flicked his change with his step as he nodded. It was a noticeable but cool sound effect. When he left the room, it was the signal that gave us the all clear to goof off, very briefly, and then we pasted on our look-busy masquerade when he returned.

He was kind. When we arrived at our room, the first room on the left from the south entrance, I saw names on the upper wall, then I spotted mine. It was colored in blue and green in perfect block letters with shadows. As I got to know my classmates, I saw their names were posted too on a sheet of colored paper with perhaps 20 minutes of stenciling and coloring. It became a talisman for me to check on Monday mornings to assure me I would have a wonderful week, and then on Fridays, I glanced at it to say, *Happy weekend, Evelyn.* This single gesture made me again aware of my identity and my placement in the social stratification of my new fifth-grade class.

Mr. Knight didn't have the enthusiasm that Mrs. O'Conner and Mrs. Monroe did. He might not have been as ancient as Mrs. Querry, closer to Mrs. Butler's age. We were a self-contained fifth grade. Our rotation based on our levels of skills would start the following year. Mr. Knight was our math and reading teacher. He proceeded through the subjects like social studies, spelling, reading, and math without a hitch. He let us sit where we wanted to as long as we didn't disturb others, so we gauged our progress quietly. We were a quiet class. We were unruly on the playground, but once we lined up in our space, some students shushed others as we waited for Mr. Knight to escort us in the building from the south entrance. This early self-monitoring made me feel like I was among caring friends who looked out for me. Being shushed was rooted in brotherhood. We must have hitched on Mr. Knight's cart very quickly and we complied to his ways. If fifth graders could fall in love in a very general sense of that special embossed word, we did. We wanted to please him. If fifth graders could feel something close to genuine caring from a teacher, we found it in ours.

Since Emerson Elementary School was a K-8 school, some of my peers had attended it since kindergarten. I felt like a haphazard forgotten guest. I saw tall, muscular seventh and eighth graders, loudly confident who clearly owned the setting. I didn't feel the protective shield of youth any longer. I was old enough to be punished, bullied in this case. I noticed the subtlety of manners, the sly glances, and the eye rolling by older girls that some fifth grade girls started to mimic. I also became aware of hostilities, from adults and students. No more did I hear, *Oh let me show you the way.* Or *Follow me.* I was pointed in a vague direction where I had to navigate on my own through what appeared to me as a two-story castle with winding corridors with possible hidden passages or rooms. I heard about a music class we would have. Even though we all moved through our destination as a herd and always dependably together, I never wanted to explore as some did when they asked for a restroom pass. Thankfully, Mr. Knight escorted us. *Don't want to lose you or for you to get lost. This is a big building*, he chuckled.

I learned early on to not be afraid to ask for help. If I was sent on an errand, Mr. Knight sent someone else with me. During these adventures, we sometimes stuck our heads into the darkened auditorium, or I stood at the base of the steps leading to Ms. Vann's art class. The ceilings were high in every part of that building. Emerson was two stories and had portables and a gorgeous playground. Instead of portable or stand-alone buildings, Emersonians called them *cottages*. I wouldn't have described it as a two-story K-8 school on Seventh Street with tall, sweeping windows or picturesque trees and rose bushes mathematically spaced on a gorgeous green lawn, a storybook school. I would have simply said, *Big. Really big school.*

One day someone pointedly whispered, *That's the nurse's office*, as we walked by a small, insignificant room. I did a double take because I thought my peer was pulling my leg. I had assumed the nurse's office was a euphemism for the principal's office. This nurse had a cot, paper cups that she administered various concoctions, or gave ice packs. Having already elevated school secretaries, I scooted the school nurse up the ladder, next to secretaries. I thought school secretaries were amazing people, operating phones with multiple buttons, receiving student and adult visitors, putting them all at ease with their usual measured cheer, someone to wave to as I happened to walk by but never stopping to talk because I didn't want to go near the nurse's office, which I believed was a promise I told myself I'd never see. I saw how far the small nurse's office was far from the principal's office, I decided I wouldn't mind making my way there, one day.

Like Garfield, the school building was dignified; it had an elegance to it. Was it the architecture, the spotlessness, the replicas of framed masterpiece paintings arrange down corridors? I hadn't visited a museum yet, but we would this school year. Emerson had a setting that invited self-control. Within the quiet enclosure, we used our quiet voices, and we mimicked adults by taking measured steps. While we were mad on the playground or walking to school, once we approached the campus, we pulled up our socks that had slipped into our heels, tied our shoelaces, yanked up our jeans, tucked in our shirts and finger-comb our hair into place.

Fifth grade had indeed a new feel to it. For those of us who transferred from Garfield, we might have felt a tad out of place. Maybe. I was also aware of having more responsibilities. I also was aware of the feminine qualities of girls who had freely made faces or flipped birdies to announce their opinions the year before, but something seemed to have happened over the summer that I had missed out on. There had to have been a fun party in a semi-lighted setting where girls learned to play quiet games and to huddle together and titter from behind hand-covered mouths. My openness and how I dashed to places stood out. I noticed using the sleeve of my shirt to mop my sweaty face was an oddity. The girls went to the restroom to wash their faces and hands and dabbed themselves dry using a cloth rolled on a loop. Up to this time, I did my business and washed my hands and walked out of the restroom with damp hands, using my jeans to dry them, or slapping the excess on my face for a quick cooling touch. It seemed an extra inconvenience to bother drying delicately on the heated cloth on rolling pins, especially in the Phoenix heat. Thankfully, some of my Garfield friends had joined me in Emerson, and if it weren't for their friendly invites to walk to school or walk home, I might have felt terribly out of place, in this new setting.

On the second day, Mr. Knight showed us where he kept the teacher answer books. *If you read the assignment, but you can't figure out the answer, here are the answers. I should warn you, however, that these are abbreviated and scanty. Should you need help, here they are.* He paused to let us digest this.

I liked that he kept the answers out in the open.

I prefer you use them to verify your answers, but I understand if you need help.

Wow, how novel, I decided. I also made a note that fifth grade was going to be a cinch. However, I quickly noticed that my pride would bar me from using the teacher answer book as often as I thought I would. Instead when we were answering questions, we pointed with our pencil to where the answer was on the pages, but the smartest person in our group, red-headed Lana, shook her head and pointed to another paragraph. Later when we checked our work aloud, Mr. Knight had us rationalize our answers by his, *How did you discover that answer?* The harder one was: *Why do you think that's right?* Or, *What makes that correct?*

When we defended our answers, Mr. Knight smiled and came to life. He trained us early by being unsmiling, but when he asked us questions, he smiled. He never completely relaxed and kicked up his feet, but seeing him smile was worth the effort of reading and re-reading and writing our responses. I was conscious of wanting to maintain his peaceful manner, and getting his approval was a worthwhile effort.

As a K-8 school, Emerson's lunch period was staggered. We lined up alphabetically, so I was one of the lead students. Mr. Knight called my name and gave me a yellow lunch card. On the end were Monday, Tuesday, Wednesday, Thursday, and Friday. When we reached the cafeteria entrance, a lunch lady with a pair of scissors snipped my lunch card as she checked off my name. We then watched women with netted hair coverings and plastic-gloves scoop food onto trays and slide on a rail them. At the end, we got our hot lunch. Mr. Knight sometimes monitored us in the cafeteria. I was ruled by recess, so I ate what I liked and gave the rest away. I wanted nothing else but to be outside in the sun. From the cafeteria, we stepped down into an enclosed courtyard. Past gates that remained opened during lunch and recess and opened onto what seemed a huge schoolyard. On the left were bleachers and farther to the left were basketball courts. To the right, a ways off, were the playground structures, swings, monkey bars, teeter totters, and right in the center, three tetherball poles shaded by a magnificent tree. When I first saw them, I thought of Monica, and I wondered where she was. Did she still have that powerful serve that had swung the ball out of my reach despite my leaps? I joined the line of girls to wait my turn at tetherball. Farther across the field in an enclosed area were more swings. The whole yard was busy with students filling the playground. It was joyous and loud, and it was nice to meet new people and reunite with friends from Garfield.

Magic had occurred over the summer. The girls had started to tower over the boys. Lana, all limbs, stood a full foot above most. She was our leader, her red hair flashing in the sun. She smiled and laughed easily. I liked her sister Shari because while the other girls adopted daintiness and soft movements and voices, Shari was the only girl who kept her normal voice. She grinned when she shot and gathered marbles or joined a fast basketball game. She might have cared about her appearance, like so many of our gender suddenly seemed to, but I held onto her company because she appeared the only normal one. I imagined that when the other girls returned to normalcy, Shari and I would be the only ones who stayed true to our identities. I did feel a heartbreaking loss of female society. Where were my comrades? Who took them and gave me shelled people with entirely different interests and behavior? I allowed Shari some slights. She might have brushed her hair occasionally because in fifth grade was when I noticed girls carried purses, another inconvenience. I wasn't quite sure what girls stored in them, but I saw hair-brushes, lip gloss tubes, and an occasional small change purse. Shari at least carried a plastic black comb that she ran through her blond shag. I didn't carry anything. I didn't see the point of brushing my hair when it would become windblown or tangled again.

Lana and Shari's little brother Ben later would become one of Dean's best friends. I did notice, for the first time, how Lana and Shari didn't share the same last name, but Ben had Shari's last name. This was perplexing me enough for me to note it, but I didn't have enough curiosity to ask how three siblings who looked alike could have two different last names. Like his older sisters, Ben was pleasant, but he was given total freedom from his grandmother, his stepfather, and mother. He stayed at our home way longer than I thought imaginable or allowable by parents. Certainly, my parents wouldn't permit my wandering from home at such late hours. Yet, Ben had a bit of charm, like my brother Dean, and my mom gave him snacks, mainly burritos made with potatoes, Spam, and green beans wrapped in her homemade bread. She gave this to Ben as she chased Dean inside. Ben was polite and cheerful—like the white version of my brother. I liked Ben, too, but in a distant manner. I had the older sister superiority. I also noticed that Dean transferred to Emerson instead of attending third grade at Garfield School. My parents must have had tremendous faith in my supervision, or decided Emerson was sufficient. We sometimes walked to school together, but often we separated to our separate groups but remained in sight of one another.

Lana and Shari's family dynamic puzzled and intrigued me. I secretly liked that when Lana's grandmother asked where she was headed, Lana sulkily answered, *The store*, but she went elsewhere. I wouldn't dare be so insolent to my mom, or my dear grandmother. I decided that the magic of living with a grandmother dwindled family loyalty to nothing, and that's why Lana treated hers with disdain. Yet, Lana was good-natured with us, her friends. I puzzled over this contradiction, as I joined Lana's entourage composed of Maria, Tiny, Dorlinda, Pamela, Seattle, Washington (named according to where they both were born), and a few others. Brigette, from Garfield, led another group that included Essie, Stella, and Santa. Though all small statured, they were a vocal group. Another band included Trish and another girl name Kelly, but not nearly as tall as our Lana. Some like Wilma, Lupe, Elaine, Karla, Diama, another girl named Beth, and I were free agents. Emerson had far more white students than Garfield. Those of us who lived south of Roosevelt stuck together, so that was true of the white students like Lana,

Shari, and Dorlinda. We often walked together homeward, our group lessening once we reached Roosevelt Street. I sometimes walked with Lana's entourage along Seventh Street beside blaring traffic, a noisier and hotter route. While I enjoyed this walk, I felt it was route due to the traffic. As much as I liked their company, I chose to walk with other students on a different path.

I found another band, with far fewer walkers, walked on Eleventh Street, a quiet, residential route shaded by orange and lemon trees. Far from the churn of traffic and blinding-hot sidewalks, I found this walk leisurely and very pretty. If we saw a lemon tree with branches overhanging the sidewalk, the fruit was free game. We picked them, and out of somewhere someone pulled out a canister of salt that we took turns sprinkling on the flesh so we could suck the the salty juice and chew the rinds. If there boys in the group, they spat chewed rinds at us as we raced from them laughing. We would not do this for long, I'm sorry to say. Just a few months earlier, I would have been one of the rind-spitting boys. Fifth grade pronounced great social change. Girls protested about small inconveniences that they'd ignored or dismissed before. I couldn't quite make sense of it yet, but I felt left behind. I felt like I had entered, uninvitingly, into the world of Ophelia or my mom, an unstated mire of layered powers.

Before and after school, we stopped at Chuck's Market, a small store with three aisles of canned goods and small dairy refrigerator in the back. I had no interest in anything but Chuck's penny candy. A nickel had value. A dime was wonderful. A quarter was heaven. I occasionally saw a dollar, but I can't recall every having one. If a fellow walker bought a soda pop, we all shared, just as we had lemons. Germs were ignored. Food sharing formed alliances or pacts. I had no compunction about sharing a piece of gum with Shari if she asked me for it. We actually took turns chewing the same wad of gum on our way to school. Of course, the sharing included shoes. I wore knockoff Converse, so when Shari wanted to play basketball, we traded shoes. I wore hers until the end of the day. When we switched, we knelt under a tree and exchanged shoes.

The walks to and from school seemed long. I asked a Native student named Renee where she lived because she caught the bus home. Her street was only three blocks south of mine. She and her brother Keith rode the school bus. Coming home earlier might just make me available for extra chores, so I decided walking home was best. Besides several students walked farther than I did.

I wondered about a lot. I wondered about the girl change. Boys remained pretty much the same, still awkward. Sometimes to contemplate this metamorphosis, I separated myself from the others. The best place to make sense of my new fifth-grade world were the swings on the eastern side of campus. An Apache student named Isaac often joined me. I couldn't explain my new fifth grade perplexities, but he smiled and politely hung by in a nearby swing and chatted. Isaac agreed with all my opinions and smiled with the corners of his mouth turned up—more so when he looked at the sun when he said, *The bell will ring soon.* His smile reminded me of the whiff of newly expelled air, that feeling of lightness, ready for the next intake. He had the look of relaxation and kindness mixed into one.

Then a strange thing happened that taught me a lesson. Just when I started to take notice of him, his attentiveness and polite interest in me, my friend Lana decided Isaac was cute. She talked about him as we walked home. She had noticed qualities about Isaac that I escaped me. His thick, thick unkempt black hair seemed more lively when Lana described it. She admired his smooth skin and *instant tan*. In her descriptions, Isaac seemed more noteworthy and attractive than he seemed to me. I realized right there on the east side of Seventh Street, with its honking and angry traffic, that Isaac was Lana's fifth-grade grade love interest. When he hung out with me, I treated him as an interest property of Lana's. I took a wide step around Isaac and his smiles.

Frankly and painfully, I admitted I didn't have the Lana confidence or learning that might make me as interesting as she was in my eyes. Probably Isaac didn't know that yet, but I certainly did. Frankly, I didn't have the freedom to wander or the courage to rebuff my grandmother as Lana did hers, to transform a playground friendship into more. I was still tucked warmly under my mom's wing, and I rather like it there, too. My appreciation for Lana outweighed my value of Isaac.

I don't think I understood the dynamics of relationships making or maintenance. I already saw the unhappy dopiness of young love. Girls sometimes wandered by themselves after a breakup or confusing conflict. When someone tried me as a confidant, the *he-said-I-said-he-did-and-I-did* rally that went beyond me. My best advice might have been *Why-not-let-it-go* because this sounds like a jack of a mess, but what did I know? Their romantic turmoil seemed fumbles at hand holding or near brushes at kissing—acts far more complicated that I could imagine. Isaac had a handsome smile, even when he was looking at the play yard, but I can't say I wanted to touch, or even brush, his hand with mine.

I was learning to recognize the invisible line of sisterhood in romantic claims. I knew the yearning of losing something that I thought was mine or the wishfulness of having something taken from my orbit, but until then, it had been a prized book or a picture. I knew what it was like to return a library book when I wanted to keep it under my pillow where I could touch it secretly after the house's molecules and light hushed.

What escaped me was that Isaac might have seen me, as a fellow Native sister. However, we never talked about Native topics, beyond, *Yeah, we Indians are always the bad guys. And we're always the ones who die before the end of the movies. Yeah.*

The *Yeah* was heavy because what else was there to say? We were two outsiders, perhaps not in school, but certainly in society. I no longer lived on my nation due to circumstances that encompassed kin, schools, and economics. My parents labored to create a combine income though my mom's was the independence of an artist, but my dad left with metal lunchbox in hand, donned in a uniform. I didn't know Isaac's family circumstances were, but his might have been similar to mine on some level. We didn't explore much in each other's worlds. We vaguely knew we would soon reside in this inevitable adult life. When we talked about movies, we often saw the same Spaghetti western that at least feature a bad but cool Pancho Villa like character. I had not seen any glamorous Geronimo or Crazy Horse characters yet in TV-land. So Isaac was content to smile and hang out, but we never broached on Native topics beyond the predictable outcomes of TV-land western depictions. But now I was well aware of the alcoholism and restlessness in Native theme, well modeled by my dad, relatives and people I saw in my urban settings. I didn't know of many Native adults in my urban setting to admire and love, as I did my *Ma Sani*, my Uncle Kee Nez Begay, and my paternal great-grandmother Lola. Rather, I had literary characters and distant adults who didn't know my name or of my existence, I admired.

In fifth grade, just as the numbers I had come to know like friends changed character when associated with different symbols, whether parenthesis, division, multiplication, square roots, powers, or less than or greater than, and the ultimate beasts, the-greater-than-or-equal-to or the-lesser-than-or-equal-to signs, my friendships with people I'd come to know had to evolve as they formed different groupings, perhaps even functions.

After ceding my friendship with Isaac to Lana's crush, I hung out with Shari. I could figure her out easily because she was like me. She wore cutoffs with roomy Ts and tennis shoes. I knew that she loved marbles and basketball more than I did, so I gave her the opportunity to take a cat-eye marble because it made her so happy. She grinned and laughed as she pocketed my cat-eye. What was the harm? I let her take the basketball from my hand as I dribbled. What's the harm in that? Of course, I never let her win so easily in tetherball, but Shari had zero interest in my favorite game. I learned compromise early. Isaac fell into the compromised field.

I certainly saw people who used to slide onto home plate during a game and dust themselves off proudly for gaining a point for their team suddenly pivot and wrinkled their noses about running across a hot field when the return-to-class bell rang. Shari and I were the only ones who seemed to like still running across. I accepted her challenge, *Race you*.

The world of my school had indeed shifted right before my unseeing eyes. Besides Shari, I didn't have anyone. She never made observations about attire, hair, eyes, or persona. I couldn't add anything to the *Jorge has pretty grey eyes* or *Did you see how strong he is?* I could only say, *Jorge's family has a small dog that waits for him by the gate*. Jorge's family dog adored him and, before he got into view, he whistled, and his dog barked happily, remaining on the porch even though it wasn't tied. That's a pretty cool trained dog. Did Jorge train his dog to do that?

As for Jorge's strength, I thought I was strong, too, but none of that mattered in the eyes of my female peers. The only person who raved about me was my *Ma Sani* when I chopped and stacked wood for as many accolades as I could secure. I decided the admirers of Jorge, Frankie, or Sandy didn't know much about them--beyond their fifth-grade handsomeness. For example, Sandy had a very nice sister who did the family laundry at the laundromat where I did. We both read our books while we waited for our family's clothes to dry. I asked her once how she kept her Converse so white. She answered, A *bucket of bleach and water and a scrub brush*. I decided that keeping shoes that white was too much bother, faintly reminding me of the process of beautifying that required time and effort.

Fifth grade also taught me I didn't know the symbols above vowels. Mr. Knight once kept us for lunch for not knowing them. I knew short and long, but the little V and sideway colon, these I didn't. When he decided to play hardball, robbing our lunch time, I finally buckled down and listened to peers and then mimicked them to have my time outside. I recall how I smiled to joined the others, and it appeared like tame fun, until Mr. Knight separated us once we got our lunch to follow him back to class and learn those sounds. That punishment was insightful on multiple levels. Mr. Knight sat at his desk to eat his lunch, and I noticed he took out a cloth napkin that he carefully draped over his lap and another that he tucked over his collar and tie before proceeding to eat. I also noticed how he spread the contents of his lunch from his lunchbox in a thoughtful manner. I still recall the trace of his smile as he unlatched his metal lunch container. It made me think of my dad, far away under the overpass on Seventh Street eating his lunch prepared by my mom. I doubt he had two napkins as my teacher did, but I saw my mom tore a section from a paper towel, folded and tucked it into my dad's lunchbox, but I also saw she sometimes used a cloth napkin. That little observation opened my eyes to class and culture. I learned just enough to spread the napkin onto my lap before starting to eat. I also noted that he didn't wolf down his food as I had watched the men in my life do. I had formed the impression that men ate faster than women. I liked sitting beside my grandmothers who both ate slowly. Often when they didn't finish their bread, they wrapped it with a tea towel and placed it on the table. In the case of my *Ma Sani*, she placed it in her jacket or windbreaker pocket. I was the later recipient of that dry bread when we under that expansive gathering and herding sheep. I don't recall all that Mr. Knight had in his lunchbox, but I did see him eat his cake first. He ate from a Tupperware-like container that he didn't appear to finish. That was also revelatory. I decided that was true wisdom: Eat what you like first.

At our desks, in the meantime, we negotiated trades from our lunches.. I gave away my dessert for orange slices. I hadn't quite adapted to the rich saucy dishes of lasagna. I was divided on Sloppy Joes, tomatoe-y sauce drenched in oily ground beef on spongy white rolls. There was no neat method of eating them. When I least tried and stopped caring, my chin and shirt front were stain free, but when I was fearful of catching food with my chin and shirt, well, invariably that's exactly what predictably happened. Clearly Mr. Knight didn't have that concern with his two carefully placed napkins. He did devour his plum with gusto, lifting his collar-napkin to catch the juice. I didn't recall having had a plum recently, and I decided to badger my mom for one on our next grocery trip.

This brief insight into teacher life also opened another room that I had never entered. I had believed that everyone of my classmates were the same, until I realized that only a distinct few who struggled with vowels and sounds that stealthily manifested in unique enunciations were asked to stay in during lunch. I saw that I was like the others: all of us were students of color. I had not yet noticed this pattern, but I recognized them as students I knew and liked. I felt the strength of that bond, not what it might have suggested about our understanding of English that our previous instructors may have failed to incorporate into their instructions. I noticed we all had attended Garfield, where many fond school memories had developed and lingered. Together we laughed at the symbols above the vowels. We made fun of them, asking, *Is it like...?* Another piped up, *Nah, nah, it's like this, you guys.* More laughter. When I glanced at the clock, I wanted out of the room to be part of the outdoor freedoms contingent. One by one, we all got serious and helped one another pronounce the right vowel sounds, so when Mr. Knight tested us again, we all single filed out and made haste for the freedom grounds.

That was my first taste of the possibility that, in a real sense my English may not have been as strong as I imagined. I also became conscious that what was considered "good

English" varied depending on context. If an adult complimented my English, I had to weigh it. Was it out of politeness? Why would someone state that in the first place? At first I answered, *Thank you*, and left it at that, but sometime during that year, I started to notice who made the comment. Invariably it was a female, a rather nicely-mannered woman, usually a mom. I decided to pay attention to what exactly prompted their observation. When I heard it from a friend's mom, then it usually meant approval. However, when a teacher said it, especially a male teacher like Mr. Knight, spoke about proper English, I took notice. One day Mr. Knight said it to us one day. He waved a sheaf of papers that we had handed in sometime earlier, and he wasn't happy.

I don't understand, students. All of you speak proper English, so why I am getting assignments written in gibberish? I'm handing these back and I want you to answer in clear English. Reread the chapter first, then answer the question. Resubmit please.

He was a kind man who jingled his coins as he walked, but now his coins didn't jingle and he'd lost his look of platitude. The clear lenses of his wired-frame glasses flashed. He then passed our the papers back to us. I waited in high anticipation, wondering where I'd gone wrong in my writing. I waited as my peers received their papers and looked glumly at the notes. Some started making corrections as soon as they received their papers, admitting fault and accepting the academic lashing. When I received mine, I looked over the paper. I didn't see any complaints in angry red. I got the usual, *Nice work*. I even turned over the paper to see instructions on re-doing my work and found none. Once everyone started on theirs, I waited awhile before pushing back my seat and walking up to Mr. Knight's wooden desk. I placed my paper before him. His face had smoothed out and he was back looking like the fifth-grade teacher we knew. He smiled, *Evelyn?*

Mr. Knight, I'm confused. How do I get this, pointing at his comment, *and have to resubmit my work?* The words hit the insides of my mouth because this was the first I'd embarked on the journey of teacher-questioning.

Oh. I see. Evelyn, your work is fine. He paused. *Only resubmit if you want to.* He dipped his chin and his lenses flashed.

I widened my eyes and shook my head slowly. If I didn't have to, I wouldn't. My teacher accepted my work. Oh, happy day! What affirmation. When I returned to my seat, I thought of pulling out my sketch pad, but on second thought I opened my social studies book to the next chapter. I joined the rest on their assembly-line work.

As kind as he was, Mr. Knight had his imperfections. At ten, I was generous with teachers, still holding onto the belief they were elevated people who acted as my parent surrogates. They were people I trusted in the far-from-perfect world I was getting to know. Our otherwise generous teacher centered on Kurt, a wimpy-looking white kid who was one of the shorter boys in our class. He had a classic, clean crew cut and pale pink skin like the color of the baby bird, we once found on the sidewalk as we walked home.

We had crowded around, crooning *Poor thing*, as we looked up at the tree, and spied a nest high up on a crook of a branch. The solution seemed easy for Jorge, who made ready to climb the tree to return the new downy hatchling to the nest. It cried out softly yet incessantly; we all knew the alarm of being small and lost. Jorge started climbing as we fashioned an open paper box from loose leaf paper that we had learned how to make sometime that year. Just when Jorge was sufficiently high in the tree, a voice called out, *Hey, what are you kids doing? Hey, get out of that tree. Now. Get down.* This voice behind a black screen didn't step outside but belonged to a yeller.

We're trying to return a baby bird to its nest, someone braved.

I don't give a care. Get out of that tree, the voice sounded. *Get off my property.*

We silently debated as our bird holder, leaped at a branch and took hold when Jorge, our climber and depositor, reached down for the paper box containing the alarmed chick.

I'm calling the cops, the voice threatened.

Hurry, we whisper-barked. Our second person then lifted the paper box up to Jorge who was close to the nest. Once he deposited the bird, Jorge grinned and started jimmying his way back down. He landed happily and slapped his hands on the legs of his jeans, and we ran away from that voice behind the screen. For a while we crossed the street when we passed by this house, but we never saw the owner of that voice.

That bird reminded me of Kurt. He was small, had translucent skin, often had red-rimmed eyes, and he didn't seem to harm anyone. He had a ready smile for everyone, girls and boys. He hung out with the other white boys. At least that's how I saw it. They lived in the vicinity and most were walkers, like us, but they didn't walk as far as we did, crossing Roosevelt Street. They crossed Seventh Street and walked in areas we never ventured into.

On the day that Mr. Knight scolded us about our less-than-acceptable work, Kurt was sit-in another pod, grinning politely as usual. I saw Mr. Knight rest his gaze on Kurt.

For another scolding, Mr. Knight centered on Kurt.

Kurt, wipe that smirk off your face.

That might have startled Kurt, but he only raised his brow, faintly. His grin didn't fly away. He only deepened it. His teeth shone, but his smile wasn't pleasant.

I'm warning you, Kurt.

So Kurt lifted his hand and wiped it across his mouth, and when he removed it, he no longer had his wild grin. I don't know if he was clowning with Mr. Knight, and I'm sure our teacher debated a bit, but then he resumed his scolding about whatever he was addressing.

Mr. Knight's scolding, almost too sharp to witness, taught me that adults I considered humane and smart could have flaws. No doubt we had a complicated love and fear of him. We never wanted to get on the bruising end of his words or his silence. Something about Kurt pestered Mr. Knight. Up to then, I thought whites preferred whites. I saw Mr. Knight's kindness to Lana and other people I saw as white, but why didn't he give the same treatment to Kurt? We didn't say anything about this, and maybe we were glad Kurt got it, but I turned this around and around in my mind, trying to break into its meaning. I don't think Mr. Knight understood it himself because he never changed or tamed his razor glances at the waif-like Kurt.

We must have had a brotherhood of sorts in our class because that experience made Kurt popular for a time. In his insignificant manner, he became the center of our attention and support.

If he had been like Owen, a white boy who called me redskin several times a week, no one might have taken notice. Owen knew the ins and outs of teacher communication. He said, *No sir. Yes sir*. He stood at ramrod attention when Mr. Knight spoke or walked by, but he knew where I stood on the authority ladder, so maybe that's why he snidely whispered, *Hey, Redskin*, when he walked past me, so quietly that only I and his constant sidekick Paul heard him. Paul snickered and laughed at the racial bullying.

Kurt was in a different category. Sandy, Miguel and others took enough of a shine to him to let him in our hand greetings. Kurt smiled and joined, and one time I even heard him laugh. That lone laugh made me smile. He wasn't a handsome boy but his laugh was a rare bird.

We weren't always a compassionate lot. When people sensed weakness, we sunk in like ravenous predators. Our clear favorite for picking on was Tiffany, whom we called Tiffy, and on our mean days, Crybaby Tiffy. She earned this nickname well before fifth grade. She was super smart, merciless in catching and correcting our errors. If she didn't get her way, she busted into a flood of tears. Hers weren't the kind that some hid by running to the restroom for walking alone to allow the dam to well over privately. Tiffy's style was to raise her voice and bellow loudly without shame and almost with a bit of pride. I know we all cried about injustices, whether about our loved ones or mean relatives, Tiffy didn't discriminate. All injustices were in the same category for her. I was amazed how out of her blue, her tears spouted. Even in my saddest moments, I couldn't coax tears. She was utterly amazing, so it was most fun to pick on her, to trip her, and rib her, and to see her cry and spout out. I could never see enough of Crybaby Tiffy cries. Later, after spring break, we watched one another, including Tiffy, cry, but then, we all cried together.

Meanwhile, at home, all had turned upside down. Something invisible haunted my mom. She would suddenly crumble and fall on her bed in tears. I didn't understand, nor did my dad, but during one of her episodes, he desperately hurried to the closest phone at a neighbor's to call for help, instructing us to pick the living room. My dad to our knowledge had never called anyone. Dean and I were paralyzed. When he returned, our dad did something we never have seen him do: pick up the odds and ends in our living room himself. He might as well have somersaulted across the living room floor or belted out in a song and dance. My mom still lay crumbled on their bed gasping. Our planetary spin had somehow altered, discolored and disappeared. If someone were to spot the beginning of the end of life, we saw it. Its crack was barely visible to the naked eye, but we felt the vibrational tremors in our marrow, tainting our security oxygen.

Soon someone knocked on our front door. Dad answered, and Dean and I scooted closer to one another. Mom had quieted some, but she was still sobbing. Since I'd never seen her so uncontained and unraveled, I didn't know what to make of her new self. In her heart, did she want to return to a faraway home and family, or to an earlier self before she accumulated what she had? I had no idea. *Whatever it is, let her breathe it out*, I prayed because I knew how a deep exhalation calmed my own aches.

Dad answered the door and welcomed into our home two men dressed in pressed suits with white shirts and ties. I'd only seen men similarly dressed in schools, in church or in politics, so it was startling to see two men dressed in this manner right in our home. Dad wrung his hands before shaking theirs, and then with stops and starts, attempted to introduce us, something I don't ever remember him doing. He must have been very upset and nervous. I suddenly wondered if I got my stammering from him. *Geez, Dad, we two are yours. How could you confuse us?* The crisp whiteness of their shirts reminded me of Sandy's sister's instruction about the bleaching of shoes.

Shortly after my dad's forgetfulness of us, the white men shook our hands and smiled broadly. One resembled Adam Cartwright from *Bonanza*. His thick black brows looked like they needed a lawn mower trimming. The other man looked like he must have lived and worked indoors 24 hours a day; he was pale and had cool hands. After introductions, they asked about my mom. They did not speak to our mother right away but depended on my dad's explanations. Quietly, they agreed to bless my mom. My only experience prayer other than my mom's has been at the church led by my *cheii*'s brother and from the pictures in Arthur S. Maxwell's Bible story collection. To hear about a blessing right in our living room was jarring but amazing.

My dad coaxed my mom from her bed and he pulled up a chair for her to sit on as the two suited men conferred quietly. Out of somewhere one produced a vial. They whispered talked and then turned to my folks. My brother Dean and I were their captive audience. Adam Cartwright look-alike asked my mom for her full name, about which my dad suddenly remembered this.He too seemed lodged in a space where he was captive because I could see him process every detail. He pronounced it beautifully, *Her name—my wife's name is Elsie Yazzie Begody*. He said this with a reverence I didn't think he had in him. Briefly I watched slides of him trailing in on a Saturday or Sunday morning red-eyed and in a defensive mood, or quietly as he made for the bathroom for a shower and then the bed for much needed sleep. I remembered his roving eyes on Ophelia and any pretty women—white, Black, Latina, or Native, easy for the picking. I don't ever remember seeing an Asian woman, but I'd have bet if my dad saw one, he would likewise forget his fatherly and husbandly station. This was an unfamiliar role for my Dad, fumbling, stammering, as he guided my mom into a seat. He visibly transformed before these men.

The pale, cool-handed white man dabbed what seemed like small droplets from the vial on my mom's crown, itself transformed into a bushy nest. Our local beauty queen no longer, she would not have embraced this as her regular Kodak moment.

Mr. Cool Hands white man secured the vial lid and placed it in the inner pocket of his suit jacket. The Adam-Cartwright-confirmed my mom's full name before they placed both hands on her crown to pray. Most of the prayers I had heard were in Navajo. My mom's mighty prayers were the most frequent ones I knew and heard.

This prayer had the intensity of my mom's. Sounds outside the room had become muffled and fallen away while the texture of the men's voices intensified. I heard every word of the prayer, but the arrangement of the words was outside my lexicon, and I didn't know what it all meant. All I knew was that my mom's agitation stopped and my dad wilted under the power of witnessing that spoken prayer. That moment sealed our membership in the Mormon church. We wouldn't be baptized until later that fall, on October 11th, after our membership lessons but the night my mom was blessed started us down that path.

The miracle was seeing my mom stand up from the chair with bounding energy and thank the men herself. If I hadn't seen it for myself, I wouldn't have believed it. What a strange evening: seeing my mom writhe on the bed, my dad run and call for help and then welcome suited strangers into our house, and seeing the vial, and hearing the blessing. Our home changed and grew in proportions that were both supernatural and sacred. This experience would change how I behaved in our small house. It took on the new definitions of what a home really was. This place where I hurried to my room to drop off my books before doing my afternoon chores, and spent hours eating at an aluminum-sided, pockmarked table could have greater meaning than I understood. How many times had I walked across the same green nylon thrift-store rug where the two white men had walked and stood as they blessed my mom? It was like opening a hidden door into a familiar room and being amazed by what the different angle revealed. We all were transported a new place within the same, familiar space. The understanding, which often floated just beyond our reach, that we were all very, very important was restored to our family.

Not quite similar but one afternoon in the early spring, we fifth graders returned from lunch to our regular afternoon reading. We couldn't help glance out the great windows that faced west. Across the fenced green lawn that defined where Emerson School ended and the outside world began, beyond the Seventh Street traffic that we somehow filtered out as we did our school work, the palm trees of Palm Lane bending and swaying at irregular degrees. Heavy, ready-tospill clouds hung onto the tiptops of the palm trees, moving vulnerably before us. If I'd had a Navajo classmate seated in my room, I would have glanced at him or her to question what the signs meant. The rumblings were so loud that Mr. Knight walked, coins jingling, across the room to shut out their menace. He could do nothing about the terrible clouds. All I could think of is how I was going to run home in this storm. I'd been instructed that during thunder storms, a person was to stay indoors—not make her way home as I would need to in an hour or two. A lightening bolt could snap, shake, and give a person a slap down like no other, sometime snatching the life out of a person. I wasn't for that. I was in the middle of fifth grade, still in single digit grade education. I knew I still had a lot to learn. We weren't even halfway through our social studies or math text.

I wasn't the only one in turmoil. None of us were reading anymore. One or two studied the pages just to avoid looking at the apocalyptic storm, but I could read the terror on their faces. Some of my peers were already torn at the seams. Crybaby Tiffy had orchestrated some in loud tears, others cried quietly. It took Mr. Knight's clear voice to corral us back from our dark alleyways of fear into his presence. Ordinarily he called us *Class*, but with us reduced to quivering, he instead said, *Boys and girls, let's count 1000, 1001, 1002, after we see the lightening to see how far away it is.* So we did. At first, we got only as far as 1005 before we heard the stampede of great hooves above us. Then we waited for another lightening and we counted aloud: 1000, 1001, 1002, and soon we counted even higher. That's when Mr. Knight said, *See it's moved away from our location. It's going north, I believe.* Amid sighs, we mopped up our tears, and humble smiles started to form. Even if we weren't sure we could trust Mr. Knight's assessment, we liked his assurances.

Some of us hadn't given it any thought that our tall, paunchy teacher could have could have been our age once. It was like looking at a picture of your mom or dad and wondering when the picture was taken, mistaking the vaguely familiar face for yourself but somehow not recognizing the setting. *Me? Yes, of course, it's me, but where was this place?* I thought Mr. Knight was ancient, but I meant no harm by this judgment.

Returning from spring break, my class gathered at our usual spot outside the southern school entrance We all were talking at once about our week hiatus from school. A few sported new T-shirts or shoes, but even though those who wore the same clothes looked a wave or two different, growing as we did at an amazing pace then.

As we waited in a line, the other two fifth-grade classes were escorted by their punctual teachers. Still we waited. When the other classes were gone from sight, we were louder and merrier even though we had never waited this long for Mr. Knight. After a minute or two, Crybaby Tiffy piped up, *Mr. Knight died of a heart attack during spring break.*

Most of us looked at her in quick anger. How dare she say such a hateful remark? Always looking for another beating, that Tiffy. *Shut up, Crybaby Tiffy. I'll give something to cry about if you don't shut your face,* someone threatened.

Tiffy didn't flinch in her conviction. I stared at her, trying to make sense of—her nervy but puzzling ways until our principal Mr. Mathis opened the outer door. Not a tall man, he looked like a miniature version of the late John F. Kennedy. His boulder-sized teeth and pleasant demeanor had deepened the smile lines around his eyes, yet I preferred to stay as far away from principals as possible. This morning he was no where near smiling. He stood so still that I thought I must have missed something he said. He had said nothing, instead waiting for us to quietly settle.

I'm sorry that Mr. Knight isn't here. If you will follow me.

I gave one one last stare at Tiffy. She was like the naysayer in a poorly plotted film. She definitely deserved a beating after school. Though I'd loved my spring break, I was glad to return to my normal day-to-day life and be under Mr. Knight's jingling-coin care soon.

The door to our classroom was open, and it was obvious our teacher was waiting inside. Mr. Mathis stood at the door as we filed in. As I approached I smiled anticipating seeing my teacher. But instead of the usual coming-into-class sounds, letting the last springy energy rustle out in chair moving and talking, my class did the opposite. Mr. Knight's desk was empty. Mr. Mathis followed us inside and again he stood before us. Sandy and Lana, who had grown beyond his stature, but didn't yet possess confidence in their height sat down silently. Red-headed Lana who ordinarily punctuated her entrance with a bouncy laugh that we loved, fell silent. No one grinned or smiled, least of all Kurt. Time had slowed and the room filled with an about-to-snap tension.

Class, I'm sorry to inform you that Mr. Knight died. He was a fine teacher. I know you will miss him.

He paused as he looked around at us.

That was the last moment we sat still as a class. In our grief, we immediately descended into a class from hell. We chased multiple subs out, and on many afternoons, Mr. Mathis had to pick up where the fleeing sub had left off. We wandered about the room, looked out the windows that Mr. Knight used to crack open to invite breezes into our class or shut when the chill crept in. We looked south and north on Seventh Street, whether with derision or seeking diversion, we became possessed. Other teachers looked at us pityingly. They poked their heads into the room and shook their heads sadly at how we had been transformed to a horrible class. We tormented Tiffy all the more frequently. Even I tripped her one day, and oh how delightful that was. She belted out loudly, and I sunk back in my chair blissfully. I became one with my wild-assed-ways class. We unleashed our greatest anger and grief on the poor substitutes. I don't recall ever seeing a male sub in those days. Only Mr. Mathis was able to settle us. He did it simply by sitting on a tall stool as he watched us work. He probably didn't believe the subs' complaints.

One classmate managed to open the window, push out the screen and pick shelled cones from some nameless plant that grew to a great height. He pried the cone apart and collected the wispy filaments within. Somehow he managed to stroke them on the young blonde-headed sub's neck. In minutes, her skin reddened and soon she was scratching invisible wisps on her face, arms, and hands. She probably scratched unnerved areas of her skin, too. She only lasted one morning. Mr. Mathis returned to us, grim but patient. If anyone was ever suspended for that prank, I didn't know. I want to believe our principal knew our ache.

The morning Mr. Mathis informed us of Mr. Knight's death, I couldn't conjure any tears. I sat dumbly in my seat. Lana, Maria, Matilda, the other Maria all wept. The boys cried, some quietly, but Owen, mean Owen, cried so openly that I felt sorry for him. Jorge who sat near me said, *My tears keep popping out. I can't stop them.*

Maybe Mr. Mathis felt he couldn't stop us, either. We all advanced to sixth grade. We weren't able to play our part in welcoming the next year's class by penning their first names in block letters, as our names had appeared on the southern wall, above Mr. Knight's desk. It took summer vacation to settle our hearts.

AFTERWORD

I omitted individual friends from my dedication because these dear people occupy a collective space apart from any other. Some have remained constant for decades, while others drift in, play a role, and move on. Each has a home in my heart and along my educational journey.

I'm convinced that those who agree to sign on as teachers agree to a calling. I observe how, on a mere morsel of supplies, they breathe life into classrooms. These humble and often bone-tired bodies surround me. Last year a new teacher showed me her PowerPoint and I asked if I could lift some ideas from her slides. She waved her hand to signal a generous "Of course!" I confess I used her ideas both in the classroom and to impress my evaluator.

I've retired from 30 years of public school service in Arizona, and am now in my second year in New Mexico public schools. I don't know how long I'll stay in the classroom. We have a heavy teaching workload and countless other assignments: operating multiple online programs for documentation; testing; professional development; teacher communications; parent communications. When my students ask for a hall pass, I still reach for small handwritten slips of paper, relics of an earlier era. I'll be in a perpetual state of learning, forever.

GRATITUDE & ACKNOWLEDGMENT

I'm currently in the middle of drafting my third book, another memoir. This one is about my initial experiences in the wage-earning world. When Joan Levitt, who helps with editing, and I texted back and forth about this topic, she said little, allowing me to wrestle with my ideas. However, when she senses what she calls a gem, she has something to say. Joan was there when this book germinated. My late husband Bo was a fierce supporter of my writing life from its inception and is very likely an even greater supporter now. The moment I shared with Bo that I wanted to write, he turned and swept his arm over my latest sewing project and said, *You can't do both.*

That same morning, I folded and stowed away my fabric and wiped down my sewing machine. Then I pulled out and charged my laptop. Bo was right. If I were to continue teaching as I pursued writing, I would have to budget my time like a miser. So I have, though not always well or wisely. Sometimes I observe my laptop neglected in the corner, and I know I need to abandon everything else and surrender to an all-nighter. I do this knowing that I'll face young adults hour after hour the next day. I'll risk energy and immunity, painfully conscious that a fighting spirit needs sleep. But choices must be made, and I have resources that come to my rescue with their power to revive.

Another person for whom gratitude is due is dear Kitty Whitman. I had originally met her twin Nell in Santa Fe, and within 30 minutes of our meeting, she'd brought up her sister Kitty. Nell transitioned in November 2021, and Kitty now occupies that honored space. Kitty and I finally met in person in the spring of 2025. What a wonderful moment that was. We have since become restaurant food-sharers and sea glass collectors on windy beaches. She has also come to my rescue as my second editor.

During one of my last visits with my maternal grandmother Lucy, I shared with her that I wanted to write. *Naaltsoos adasliil*. I used what I constructed in Navajo for writing, and it made no sense to her. She smiled patiently asking, *Don't you know how to write?* She understood writing to be the act of picking up a pen and scribbling a note, while I meant book-writing. Thanks to her, writing has become a process of scribbling notes to myself, not at all the herculean undertaking it might have been. On this past summer's travels to sacred sites in France, I left behind my laptop and composition book, drafting *The Spirit of Work* on my phone gmail as we hastened along by bus or van to caves and other holy sites. This less formal act of drafting was in keeping with my *masani* Lucy's vision of my writing.

While Navajo is my first language, I don't read or write it. So most of the Navajo you read or saw in this book was gained through the *Conversational Navajo Dictionary* assemble by Garth A. Wilson. This true sized pocket book has been a great resource. Another is *English to Navajo Dictionary* compiled by Robert W. Young and William Morgan. It's not a question of if I made mistakes, I have. I first removed all markers, and I reduced the Navajo to letters. Someone might cry that I don't have Navajo in this book. That's fair. For the learned and diligent student, I apologize that this book isn't a Navajo language study. However, when I needed a phrase spelled out, I turned to various people. I must include Evelyn Johnson, who helped me with *haisha niszagi yiyiiaal?* That question I posed my dad showed him his doings were now seen by me. I keep that question attached to my laptop to remind me what am I witnessing and the greater, how am I being witnessed? Speaking of that, when Evelyn Johnson and I talked, I said, I *should have used, naaltsos dawoltaigii aaas liil*— referring to that moment with my *masani* Lucy. Evelyn Johnson suggested another sentence, altogether better, but I wouldn't have constructed it.

Foremost in all this are silent reflections that take the form of my two fourth-grade granddaughters, Mason and Evan, whose own educational meanderings break ground beside my own.

AN EXCERPT FROM *THE SPIRIT OF WORK*

To be released in 2027

Campsite Clerk:

I didn't have a driver's license yet, and I could easily ride my bike to work at the fast-food restaurant, but I applied for other jobs anyway. Soon I got hired at a trading post where Native jewelry, rug weaving supplies, ranching needs, and even some food items were sold. My mother drove me for the few days I worked there. I spent much of my time talking with the manager-owner, a friendly man who demonstrated his belief in company loyalty by rescinding his offer of work to me when his former employee returned. I was a college student, a temporary hire, and his previous employee had a family to support, so I was more than willing to give up my position. But I was also relieved to exit the trading post because being there reminded me of the skewed relations between the trading post merchant and the Navajo families who traded there. Many Navajo families depended on what the trading post merchant stocked, so when he inflated prices, his customers bought without complaint. When I surrendered my job, I planned never to return there, not even for a look-see. No more friendly chats about why Mormons didn't drink coffee, even decaffeinated. Or how the cost of a Navajo rug or jewelry was calculated to give the friendly merchant a sizable advantage. It was another reminder of why and how my mom would never make a profit on her rugs or jewelry. That short stint left me with a bad taste in my mouth. I was ready to find another job, hopefully one I could once again get to on my bike.

In a stroke of luck, I was hired as a campground store clerk, where I found I could operate the noisy register with some semblance of competence. It helped that my supervisor was patient and modeled what I needed to do, speaking to me in a low voice as I watched. Then she stood by to observe, to cheer, or to correct me in the same quiet way.

I saw a bit of myself in her manner. Maybe it was shyness, although she talked in that same even tone with customers and with her tall, graying husband Buddy. I called my supervisor by her first name, Pam, though I was not as informal with her husband. He and I didn't interact much. He was busy maintaining the campsite for campers, who seemed to come in droves, as though they had traveled together there in a caravan.

I quickly mastered the register and the codes for types of campers: cabins, rigs, small or large, tent users. Once I entered the store, I usually stayed there for the duration of my shift. I hadn't expected to be busy, but I was, and having my hands full felt good. I worked on one side of the counter unless I was dusting, wiping the windows or counter, or running to locate merchandise that we couldn't find. I greeted campers, who shared where they'd driven from or how many miles they'd traveled that day or where they were headed. They seemed relieved to enter a cool refuge from the sweltering heat along the I-40 ribbon. I discovered that some had traveled along the familiar roads south of Holbrook, but most were I-40 travelers going east or west. On the wall was a map that helped me aim travelers toward the next campground.

One of my tasks was selling campground memberships. Pam and I, in a friendly competition, bet each other we'd sell a certain number of memberships each day. The last time I'd been a salesperson was as a newspaper girl years before, but now I was safely behind the counter, not knocking on doors. It was easier to smile and tease with strangers who I'd never see again, and that emboldened me. My new assertiveness showed in my summer sales numbers, and I knew I would work there until fall semester began.

One day, Pam and I offered an older traveler a camp membership in perfect unison, bursting into laughter as we concluded our appeal. He smiled broadly, likely enjoying the attention of two women, and nodded to me after an appreciative gaze at pretty Pam with her sensible Peter Pan hairstyle, propped up sunglasses, and practical smile. He said, "I'll take one from you, little lady." I didn't care that I was reduced to "little lady" and all the baggage it carried. I was after that commission. Selling memberships kept me on my toes because for each one I sold, I earned one dollar. It was nice to have a few dollars folded into my pocket when I finished the shift. Pam always made a big to-do as she counted out my daily commissions, saying, "I think that would've been mine if I hadn't answered the phone," or "Clever, clever, Evelyn."

I liked the wholesome nature of my supervisor and workplace. I finally had what I imagine must be a common workplace dream: a kind supervisor who had confidence in my work. I'm sure I made mistakes, but Pam was gentle and gracious, and I think I absorbed some of her belief in me. After my other summer jobs, I'd found an oasis. It motivated me to do more than was required, like straightening the mats, aligning store goods, and standing as tall as I could when I conversed with campers after welcoming them. I was selling something that was good for travelers and for me, a lifetime camp membership with real benefits for a few dollars. I added that the membership would pay for itself in two more camp visits. I don't know if that's still offered anymore, but it was fun to sell what I believed was a fantastic deal.

To steer my way into offering the membership, I'd say, "Would you have your campground membership so I can give you your site for the reduced price of ____? No membership? Well, we can solve that for ____, which will give you that same reduced rate in the next campground," as I pointed to the next site on that trusty wall map.

When a traveler already had a membership, I lauded her smart travel investment with a nod. I said, "For having your membership, you'll enjoy the rate of _____ for your stay with us tonight." Some travelers actually stayed an extra night after I shared local tourist sites with them: Painted Desert, Petrified Forest, or Meteor Crater. I also mentioned the

Hopi villages and the dinosaur tracks in Tuba City. I added Springerville, where the actor John Wayne supposedly lived. I always mentioned beautiful Flagstaff and Sedona, Camp Verde and Strawberry, Arizona. These were places I liked and wanted to visit again.

My experience was no longer with hungry restaurant-goers or fast-food customers. These were vacationing travelers, about whom I knew little. I had no experience planning a vacation or even taking one planned by someone else. I couldn't imagine the expenses of traveling: gasoline, food, camping costs, and unfortunately for some, vehicle repair costs. I was unencumbered by a driver's license, as I still viewed driving, like cooking, as a tiresome chore. I marveled at the wholesale acceptance of driving. I can't recall whether I had read Steinbeck's *Travels with Charley* yet, but I envied anyone who visited all the places I located on the map. I didn't want to drive but I wanted to see and experience each destination. That wish must have shone in my face as I congratulated the travelers for making it to our campground. They may not have felt they had achieved anything, but I clearly saw otherwise. As I stood with my feet planted at the cash register each morning, travelers were whizzing along the highway to or from Albuquerque or Williams or Flagstaff. "Don't forget the famous natural wonder, our Grand Canyon!" That was the beauty of the job. We offered humble comforts, a place to park and hook up vehicle lines so visitors could pull out lounge chairs and watch the sunset after cleaning up a little.

Guests were pleased when I shared our evening campsite cookout time and short menu. Most travelers were content with grilled hamburgers and hotdogs prepared by young people, followed up by campsite games and stories. To others I recommended local eateries. My enthusiasm (including towards my former fast-food restaurant) was genuine; I never smirked or demeaned my valuable training grounds.

At times, I glimpsed into people. When a couple registered, I assessed who I should speak to, looking back and forth, smiling at both. If the husband was the money handler, I made sure to pay attention to the wife during the transaction. If my membership offer was turned down, I nonetheless extended a welcome and thanked guests for visiting. I really wanted them to enjoy their stay. If I had sour customers, I made my sales pitch as efficient as possible and wished them a restful evening. After working in less-than-ideal circumstances, I knew the importance of even small displays of gratitude.

Sometimes during a quiet spell I'd listen to travel stories. If Pam was the intended audience, I listened quietly from the sidelines. A benefit of the job was meeting people from all over. Most travelers were from the upper Midwest or Midwest, and their recreational vehicles were still a novelty to me. I had the pleasure of traveling when I rode in an RV from Phoenix to San Diego and up to Manti, Utah, but it still represented traveling in style and comfort.

Then one day a man checked in who struck me as unusually attractive. I was still working out what attractive meant and who and how this term applied to men. I was introspective enough to know that I prized a few qualities; I admired someone well-spoken, kind, patient, with clean hands and a bookish way (because what was I going to talk about except what I knew?), and quiet. Here he was. I was especially aware of his tentative, careful smile, was though he didn't use it too much. I was at full alert. This was a first for me.

When I sold the man his card, I requested his name and address, and he smiled. "An Oakie from Muskogee." This struck my funny bone and I emitted a low chuckle. Brand new to this dance and hardly skilled, I tried my hand at flirting, scoring low despite my intentions. I did my best though, and he smiled appreciatively. I wanted to continue to chat, but one after another, travelers entered and waited to be checked in, curtailing my efforts.

Since this was a new experience, I was baffled at the way my body was reacting. I wondered if this man felt one iota of what I did. It defied reason to be so attracted to someone I hardly knew. I spent the rest of my shift analyzing this first crush. Later, he stopped by again, this time wearing a plaid short-sleeved shirt and looking just as handsome to me as before. I believe he asked me about local food options, but by then my tongue was tied. All I could do was smile mindlessly, more proof of the meager extent of my experience. Adding to my confusion was the fact that I wanted to keep my reputation unblemished for future work, and Holbrook was a town with only two traffic lights. At least two Holbrook residents attended BYU and I still was active in the LDS church, so this was the end of the road for me.

The next morning, I tried to seem nonchalant with Pam. "Anything exciting this morning, Pam?"

"Nope. Except that guy in the plaid shirt returned and hung out. I should have scheduled you sooner, so you could say goodbye to him."

I was silenced. I hadn't known I was so readable. I realized that my response to him, albeit wordless, had been a loud, corny broadcast for all to observe, and that if Pam had noticed my predicament, so had store customers and so had he. Thank God I was new to the world of romance and not a risk taker. I didn't want to disappoint Pam or myself. Words that had been imprinted at birth had never faded: Remember who you are. Much later, I wouldn't care who I was, but I was to be young and inexperienced for a while longer.

I smiled. "Yes, he was cute. And probably headed to Flag by now."

My reflexive use of the word cute hinted that I wasn't ready to deal seriously with men. I was still young enough to cover my face with my notebook by holding it parallel, hiding an Oh my God expression on my face. I sometimes did that for laughs when my friends stooped to rating the physical features of guys. I also admit to occasionally using the notebook for concealment when I shot a friend a glance of *Are you kidding?* A look of *No, I don't see what you're worked up about.*

I appreciated Pam for letting my crush land gently and never mentioning it again.

My summer ended in an unusual way. I happened to telephone my college roommate, who asked me where I was because the semester had begun. That unexpected, visceral jolt led to a flight in a Cessna over Heber, Arizona. The pilot who let me hold the control and steer the plane gave me a story to recount to my friends back on campus. It was my first time flying in a small four-seater and then in a much bigger plane from Phoenix to Salt Lake City. A friend picked me up at the airport and asked me how my summer was. There was no simple answer. I was far too slow for fast food. The trading post was a rude whiff of history, past and present. The campground was... and here I could only smile.

www.ingramcontent.com/pod-product-compliance
Lightning Source LLC
Chambersburg PA
CBHW021144160426
43194CB00007B/688